OLD MULKEY

A Pioneer Plea for the Ancient Order

History of the Mill Creek Church of Monroe County, Kentucky

BY

LOY R. MILAM

P.O. Box 81
Tompkinsville, Kentucky 42167
1996, 2014

© Pioneer Paths Publishing, 1996, 2014. All rights reserved. No part of this book may be reproduced, except in printed form as a matter of reference. Printed in the United States of America.

ISBN 978-0-692-23705-2

"Finally our light will shine and truth will prevail. Indeed, brethren, we have reason to rejoice that notwithstanding the floods of opposition and torrents of abuse that have poured forth from various quarters, yet truth is prevailing. Gospel light is shining. Error and sectarian bigotry is in many instances giving way; and the Kingdom of the Redeemer is spreading. . ."

John Mulkey

OLD MULKEY

Artwork by: Tony Bishop

A Pioneer Plea for the Ancient Order

History of the Mill Creek Church of Monroe County, Kentucky

Loy R. Milam

Table of Contents

Introduction

Chapter 1

A Step Back Toward the Old Paths 1-18

Chapter 2

Formation of the Mill Creek Baptist Church 19-38

Chapter 3

Religious Storm Clouds Gathering 39-56

Chapter 4

The Spreading of the Mill Creek Church 57-74

Chapter 5

John Mulkey's Hard Decisions 75-92

Chapter 6

After the Division of 1809 93-110

Chapter 7

The State of the Restoration 111-132

Chapter 8

The Passing of an Era 133-138

Chapter 9

The Next Generation 139-154

Appendix A

John Mulkey's Circular Letter to the Churches A1-A16

Appendix B

Minutes of the Mill Creek Church (1798-1806) B1-B72

Appendix C

Miscellaneous C1-C10

Appendix D

Bibliography D1-D3

A History of the Mill Creek ("Old Mulkey") Church
Tompkinsville, Kentucky

Introduction

In the small rural community known as Vernon - at the extreme southeastern tip of Monroe County, Kentucky, near the Kentucky-Tennessee border - is the grave of John Mulkey. The old headstone bears this inscription:

> John Mulkey
> A faithful preacher
> of the gospel of Christ
> Born
> Jan. 14, 1773
> Died
> Dec. 13, 1844

John is buried next to his beloved wife, Elizabeth, on a lonely and isolated hillside just off Kentucky Highway 216, on the property once owned by the Mulkeys.

Their graves are some 12 miles southeast of the church they helped establish in the late 1700's; then known as the Mill Creek Baptist Church. The church, later known as the "Old Mulkey Meeting House", two miles south of Tompkinsville, is now a Kentucky State Shrine, so dedicated in November, 1931.

John Mulkey is best known for the stand that he took, along with his brother Philip, which resulted in a division of the Mill Creek Baptist Church on November 18, 1809. But there is much more to the story.

Not only were the Mulkeys largely responsible for the spread of religion in Southern Kentucky, Northern Tennessee, and later in Southern Illinois, but they were also among the first to take a stand for the *Ancient Order of Things* in the early 1800's.

It is for that purpose that this book is being written. Much more needs to be said concerning the Mulkeys, and much more needs to be revealed about the Mill Creek Church.

In addition to the original *Minutes of the Mill Creek Baptist* Church, many historical documents have been preserved from this period involving Kentucky's religious history. However, few of those documents are within easy access of the general public, and never has the bulk of this historical information involving the Mulkeys and the Mill Creek Church been collected together under one title.

Such is the aim of *Old Mulkey: A Pioneer Plea for the Ancient Order*.

Through its pages, this book will detail the establishment of the Mill Creek Baptist Church in the late 1700's, and show how that church would become a leading force in what church historians would later call the *Restoration Movement*.

Not only will the book retrace the steps of the Mulkeys, and others, who left eastern Tennessee in the late 1700's and made their way into southern Kentucky and Mill Creek, but it will also show how the church soon spread its influence by extending smaller *"arms"* or *"branch"* churches into the area, these churches also playing a part in restoration history.

In passing, we will also take glimpses of the *Restoration Movement* as a whole, and show the role the Mulkeys played in the effort to restore New Testament Christianity to a divided religious world.

It will not, however, be the purpose of this book to rise up any man, or any group of men, as a banner. The affections of the church - past, present, and future - must center on our Lord Jesus Christ and the sacrifice that he made. He must, in all times, be the sole object of our devotion, the spiritual head of that body of which we are members (the church), and His divine Word our one and only true guide in all matters pertaining to religion. May we wear no name but His, and prize it above every other name that is named under heaven, forever and ever.

It is the author's hope that this work will help inspire within those who read it that same spirit with which the pioneer preachers of the past conducted their lives; that we might share the attitude that John Mulkey revealed in his *"A Circular Letter Addressed to the Christian Churches in the Western Country"*; [printed by] J. A. Woodson, Glasgow, Ky. 1821:

> "...Dear Brethren, let us bear all things with patience and resignation, knowing that men are not to be our judges; let us be sincerely thankful for the late revival of God's work among us, and steadily cherish the same and be steadfast, unmovable, always abounding in the work of the Lord, all the powers of darkness will be engaged to check this glorious work; and one thing will certainly be aimed at, and that will be to draw your attention to other subjects, and if possible to keep you from suitable engagements for the salvation of precious souls. The instruments that God makes use of in carrying on his work will be as marks for the enemy to shoot at from every quarter. But if we keep our eye fixed on the Savior they can do us no harm, but will often unintentionally do us good. For my own part I can truly say these things have sometimes been a great comfort to me; and when reproaches and slanders have been flying, thick on every side, my soul has been happily feasting on the love of God and a spirit to pity and pray for my persecutors, and sometimes my friends have thought that I should certainly be overwhelmed. I could still say with Paul that none of these things move me, neither count I my life as dear to myself. So that I may finish my course with you and the ministry, and that I may have received the Lord Jesus to testify the Gospel of the Grace of God. Again I say with the same servant of God, after the way they call heresy so worship I the God of my fathers believing all things that are written in the law and the prophets.
>
> And now, brethren, I commend you to God, and the word of his grace, which is able to build you up, and give you an inheritance among all them that are sanctified. The grace of our Lord Jesus Christ be with you all. Amen.

I am your servant, For Jesus' sake, John Mulkey"[1]

To those early pioneer Christians this book is dedicated. May we never forget the sacrifices they so willingly offered in search of truth.

Loy Milam
Tompkinsville, Kentucky
February, 1996

---

[1] John Mulkey, *"A Circular Letter Addressed to the Christian Churches in the Western Country"* [printed by] J.A. Woodson, Glasgow, Ky. 1821, (Copy in Christian Theological Seminary Library, Indianapolis, IN).

A History of the Mill Creek ("Old Mulkey") Church
Tompkinsville, Kentucky

Chapter 1

A Step Back Toward the Old Paths

The division which took place at the Mill Creek Baptist Church, as recorded in their minutes of August, October, and November of 1809, was not prompted by ill will among the membership, nor was it brought about because of selfish personalities. It was, rather, two sides that made their stand for what they believed to be the truth.

On the side of the minority, led by Elder John Wood, it was a decision to remain loyal to Baptist doctrine and the Articles of Faith they had adopted under the Stockton Valley Association.

For the majority, led by John and Philip Mulkey, it was an earnest plea for a return to the pattern of the church of the New Testament. Theirs were but two of numerous voices that were being heard throughout the religious world; voices that were pleading for Christians everywhere to lay aside all the man-made machinery in religion, and return to the *"Bible alone"* as their only true guide.

John Mulkey, minister of the Mill Creek Baptist Church, found himself at the heart of the controversy. But Mulkey desired unity, not division. He had voiced his ideas concerning restoration, and as a result, had been taken to trial by some in the Mill Creek Church, backed by the Stockton Valley Association.

Consequently, *"helps"* (men) were brought in from surrounding churches, also aligned with the Stockton Valley Association, to try and sort out the controversy. But their efforts resolved nothing in the matter. After much debate, it was finally the ruling of the *"helps"* that they would leave the Mill Creek Church to settle their differences themselves, in hopes that some solution could be reached where the membership could live together in peace.

In his *"A Circular Letter Addressed to the Christian Churches in the Western Country,"* printed by J.A. Woodson, Glasgow, Ky. 1821, John Mulkey revealed the events leading up to the division of the Mill Creek Church that took place in November, 1809:

> ...At the August meeting in the year 1809, myself and my opponents finding that we could not settle our differences, among ourselves, agreed to call on five of the neighboring churches, to aid us. The following October was the time agreed upon. They accordingly attended, by their delegates, took their seats and acted in conjunction with the church. The brethren, who considered me in error, then proceeded to exhibit charges against me - respecting my doctrinal views - my manner of preaching, etc. And indeed the way that some of them seemed to view my doctrines, it looked like I had gone far from the truth. However, I attended to each charge distinctly, and honestly pointed out my own views of those doctrines; and then proceeded to defend myself and my doctrines, as well as I at that time was able. And when I had gone through, and every subject was sufficiently investigated, the question was then put by the acting moderator (Elder Robert Stockton), *"For all who justify brother John Mulkey, to hold up their right hand,"* - and the majority was large in my favor. Consequently no more could be done against me at that time. And the helps that visited us returned, and left our affairs unsettled.
>
> On the second Saturday in November we met again; and after meeting was opened, I proposed to the brethren, that we drop our disputes, and try to bear with each other, and live in peace, and perhaps we might, in time, come to a better understanding. But this proposal was utterly refused - and it was replied *"never till you come*

back to the ground you started from." Thinking the impossible, agreeable to my present views; and being wearied with contention, I made another proposal, as the last alternative. And that was, if we could not live together in peace, that we agree to part in peace and each party do as well as they could. To this proposition I do not recollect one dissenting voice. And so the division immediately took place, and my opponents so far ratified the motion for the division, that they then called on all who were determined to stand to their old constitution, to come forward and have their names enrolled. I also called on all who felt like withdrawing from all human rules and man-made laws, to remove and give place to our brethren, to proceed in their own way. We accordingly did so; and I verily consider we were thus separated by mutual consent of parties; and from that day I have never considered myself a member of the Baptist Church - having dissented and left them on account of these rules and their manner of trying to enforce them; which to me appeared calculated to prevent free enquiry and to lord it over my faith.

Thus I was compelled to dissent or hypocritically conceal my real views of the Gospel. I can honestly say, I did love the brethren, and I do not feel like I should have left them, if I could have lived with them in peace, and the enjoyment of my religious liberty, at the same time. We who had withdrawn agreed to meet on the next Saturday. We met accordingly, and after solemn prayer to Almighty God for his direction and presence, we proceeded to enquire what plan we were to pursue.

After much deliberation and free conversation on every subject that came under our view, we finally concluded that all human creeds and confessions of faith were the works of fallible man and consequently they were imperfect and contradictory to each other and also that they had been the cause of many, if not most of the divisions in the church of God; likewise that they all had their zealous advocates, and, of course were calculated to divide Christians, and keep them apart. And further, believing that Christ is the great head of the church and King of Zion, the only Christian lawgiver, and that he had given a sufficiency of laws, rules and regulations, for the government of his church and people. We proceeded to unite ourselves as a Christian Society, agreeable to our best views of the Gospel; having, as we hoped first given to our Lord - we then gave ourselves to each other, by the will of God, to be subject to Christ and to each other in the Gospel, taking the Holy Scriptures as the only rule of our faith and practice, we therefore receive all whom we believe Christ has received, with the exception only of such as have been excluded from other societies, for immoral conduct; in that case we esteem it our duty, first to confess their faith to their brethren whom they offended: but if any are cast off using this religious liberty, we freely receive them, - believing that Christ has made them free, and that liberty of conscience is a right that God has conferred on his intelligent creatures and none has the right to take it from them, seeing that they are to account to God alone, for their religious conduct. Thus we have lived together in peace and brotherly love, generally speaking, and have in no instance found any deficiency in the sacred rule we have adopted, but have reason to thank God and take courage.[1]

Modern Baptist historians offer these comments in support of those members of the Mill Creek Church who opposed Mulkey:

> After a few years, John Mulkey seemed to have adopted the theology of Barton W, Stone. The main point of difference between Stone and the Baptists was over the influence of the death of Christ on God. The Baptists were afraid that Stone and Mulkey's doctrine tended to deism by reducing the death of Jesus to the level of the death of other men. Stone feared that the substitutionary theory of atonement was so contrary to the true nature of Christianity as to be itself a cause of infidelity. He believed that the alternative was the moral influence theory of atonement. The moral influence was exerted on man, and

---

[1] E. Clayton Gooden, *A Fork in the Road*, Original 1821 letter reprinted in its entirety, pp. 199-211, (Copy in Christian Theological Seminary Library, Indianapolis, IN). This letter will be included in its entirety in the appendix of this book.

not on God. The death of Christ had a "moral tendency" to lead men to repentance. The other side attempted to expose Mulkey as a deist and an infidel on the question. They were unable to see any merit in the moral influence theory of atonement. To his opponents, Mulkey had reduced the death of Christ to the level of martyrdom.

This doctrine drew a bold challenge from a large percent of the membership [of the Mill Creek Church], who regarded it as a doctrine contrary to the Christian religion, and boldly charged Mulkey with being a heretic. This accusation tormented heated arguments and unrelenting stands taken by [the] membership. Every effort made to bring about reconciliation of the membership failed.

Finally Mill Creek Church decided to call on five of the neighboring churches to help settle the matter at the October 1809 meeting. The delegates from the churches attended and during the meeting which ensued, Mulkey pointed out his views on several doctrines. It is known that he was strongly opposed to Unconditional election but whether he was explicit on his views of the atonement at this time is not known. He afterwards stated that he defended himself and his doctrines... *"as well as I at that time was able."*

An immediate result of the meeting was that the majority of the committee was in favor of Mulkey. At the moment when Mulkey's opponents thought that they had proved the charges against him, he had managed to convince the committee that he was sound in the Baptist doctrine. However a loud blast had been sounded against him and though he assumed the air of the victor, he soon discovered that the "Gileadites took the passages" before him.

The confusion was not settled. The membership wrangled and disputed, getting farther apart all the time and more determined to endorse or not endorse Mulkey. Finally, in November 1809, the dilemma through which the members had passed, was cleared up by making a division of the church members. It was while a representative number of the church were attending and a proposition was made that those who endorsed Mulkey's doctrine were to walk through one of the doors of the building, and all who opposed the doctrine of Mulkey were to walk out the other door of the building.

The proposition was also made to count the members who followed each deacon out and the deacon who had the largest number of members, he and his members were to retain the building.

The count disclosed that those who favored John Mulkey drew a majority and thereby gained possession of the building...[2]

The actual minutes of the Mill Creek Church don't add much light to the controversy, as they do little more than state the facts:

> August, Second Saturday, 1809 - Charges exhibited against Brother John Mulkey in consequence of which the church agrees to send for helps to assist us at our October meeting.
>
> October, Second Saturday, 1809 - Church met agreeable to appointments with the helps and proceeded to hear the charges exhibited against Brother John with other charges of like nature, and when again hearing the charges exhibited and debated, we then concluded that he denies the essential doctrine of the Gospel, such as denying in our esteem that Jesus Christ satisfied the demands of law and justice for his people, or died as our surety, or that any man is saved by the righteousness of Jesus Christ imputed to them, also finally, for treating the church with contempt and going away and leaving us in our unpleasant situation.
>
> November, Second Saturday, 1809 - Church met and a division took place, and those names above written [no names were ever written - there is an empty white space between the October and November minutes]. John Mulkey explains the reason for the names being omitted in his Circular Letter of 1821; [see Appendix A, pages A-7 and A-8 in this book.] declared that they would no longer remain under the

---

[2] Cawthorn, Warnell, *Pioneer Baptist Church Records of South-Central Kentucky and the Upper Cumberland of Tennessee 1799-1899*, p. 436.

constitution of this church and withdrawn [sic] from us, consequently, are no more of us.³

E. Clayton Gooden, in a small pamphlet distributed at the Old Mulkey Meeting House State Shrine, described the division in this manner:

> *"Now all you who believe as I do, follow me out the west door."* The words reverberated through the rough-hewn beams of the Mill Creek Baptist Church. It was Saturday morning, November 18, 1809. The congregation of some two hundred had gathered for the last time; and the words of John Mulkey were like a broad axe splitting the timbers of the Baptist traditions from top to bottom. All across Kentucky, Ohio, Tennessee and South Carolina, there were rumblings of discontent. Congregations were declaring themselves *"Separate"* or simply *"Christian Churches."* The restoration plea was being heard throughout the Western Reserve. And fervent revivals brought thousands to a great awakening of religion on the American frontier.
>
> John walked slowly to the right of the long pulpit that stood on the north side of the building. Approaching the low door at the west end of the church, he bent slightly to clear the lintel and stepped out into the crisp air of the autumn morning. A snow had fallen leaving the ground a deep rust sprinkled over with a fine covering of white that resembled sugar. Gusts of wind were now blowing the frozen granules across the wooded cemetery where several Revolutionary War veterans lay resting from their struggle to win their country's independence. John looked out across the rough-hewn stones. He was trying to win some independence too... He wondered if the price would be as dear...
>
> Presently, a few of the congregation closest to the west door began to rise from their puncheon pews. Hannah Pennington, sister of the famous Kentucky explorer Daniel Boone, along with Joseph Gist, a brother to the first white man to set foot in Kentucky, Nathan Breed,

---

[3] *Minutes of the Mill Creek Baptist Church*, Book Two, August, October, November, 1809.

Obediah Howard, and William M. Logan crossed the threshold and stood with Brother Mulkey in the small clearing. Others followed until one hundred-fifty of the two hundred present stood with their preacher in the gray light of a cold November morning in the county of Barren, the new state of Kentucky, some two and a half miles south of a small community called Tompkinsville.

The other fifty slowly filed out the east door of the church and stood talking quietly as if their plans were already made. Within half an hour they moved out toward their horses and buggies, and were last seen in a procession moving toward Tompkinsville. Within another six months a new Baptist church would be built, and a new congregation organized.

In the meantime, John Mulkey, the man with the majority, was in the center of a religious controversy that would lead to the founding of the largest group of Christians ever organized on American soil.[4]

Gooden's account is obviously colored with novel-style writing, but is based upon historical facts, and perhaps gives us a very realistic view of the events.

The controversy that confronted the Mill Creek Baptist Church was a dispute that hundreds of churches across the country would be forced to face in the early part of the 1800's. It would be replayed, not only in other Baptist churches around the country, but in similar form among the ranks of the Methodists, Presbyterians, and almost every other religious body in America.

In order to clearly understand the issues that faced the membership at Mill Creek, one must first become acquainted with the Restoration Movement as a whole. Then, and only then, are we capable of making our own decisions.

---

[4] E. Clayton Gooden, *The Old Mulkey Meeting House, John Mulkey: The Man With A Majority*.

Birth of the Restoration Movement

[5] By the turn of the 19th century, religion in America began to undergo a series of developments as the freed colonies broke away from the tyrannical yoke of the established Church of England and began to flex their spiritual muscles in unison with their newly- found civil liberties.

To say that these movements were calculated, and in every respect, true to the divine standard of truth, would be to attach to them a success that wasn't always the case. But step by step, men were coming out of darkness and into the wonderful light of God's truth.

The revolt of the American colonies in the late 1700's was as much for religious freedom as it was for political freedom. Under the tyranny of George III, the established religion in the pre- Revolutionary War days was the Established Church - the Church of England. All others were looked upon with disfavor, and persecution was seldom absent. The clergy of the Established Church ruled the colonies with an iron hand. Anyone who failed to attend one church service without an allowable excuse was fined one pound of coffee. Missing a month resulted in a fine of fifty pounds. No man could sell his tobacco until the local preacher gave his permission, and before that was done, the minister's portion was collected out of the first and best tobacco.

The Act of Uniformity of 1642 made it law that all ministers must conform to the orders and constitution of the Church of England and were not otherwise permitted to teach or preach, publicly or privately.

One would naturally conclude, then, that after the Revolutionary War ended, religion would immediately abound throughout America because of their new-found freedom. But, actually, the exact opposite was true.

When the war was ended, the clergy's salaries were largely abolished owing to the fact that the church was no longer state supported from

---

[5] Much of the following historical information is expanded from the author's work under the head of *The Restoration Messenger*, printed weekly in the *Tompkinsville News*, Tompkinsville, Kentucky, beginning in late 1995. For a more in-depth look at this period see Earl Irving West's, *Search for The Ancient Order*, Vol. 1, Chapter 1 (Early Beginnings).

taxation. As a result, most clergymen returned to England, leaving the people in spiritual destitution. Due to the lack of preachers, the Lord's Day became a day of pleasure, and most meeting houses were deserted.

The "Great Revival" Under James McGready

One of the first indications of renewed interest in religion was the *"Great Revival"* in Logan County, Kentucky in late 1799 and early 1800 under the preaching of James McGready.[6]

McGready was born about 1760 in western Pennsylvania, but in 1778 his Scotch-Irish Presbyterian parents moved the family to North Carolina. Several years later McGready returned to Pennsylvania to study with two respected Presbyterian evangelists, Joseph Smith and John McMillan. Under their tutelage McGready became a scintillating orator, and, being licensed to preach in 1788, he set out for his home in the North Carolina Piedmont. On his way through Virginia he chanced to visit Hampden-Sydney College which at that time was in the midst of a memorable student religious revival.

Having established himself in Guilford County, North Carolina, McGready began an intensive revival campaign with hard-hitting sermons concerning hypocrisy, materialism and sin.

McGready's efforts were divided in their effect; he touched the hearts of many and sent them fleeing from the wrath of God, but in the process, he put his own life in danger as he made many enemies who threatened him with death if he did not cease his guilt- provoking preaching. Blood on the pulpit later convinced McGready to seek more peaceful fields in the west.

Consequently, McGready moved to Logan County, Kentucky in late 1796. The following January, he took charge of three small churches - Red River, Muddy River, and Gasper River.

During the bleak winter of 1797-1798 he was able to get his sparse congregations *"to observe the third Saturday of each month, for one year, as a day of fasting and prayer, for the conversion of sinners in Logan County, and throughout the world."* In addition they promised to spend a half hour on Saturday evenings and Sunday mornings *"in pleading with*

---

[6] The following information relating to the ministry of James McGready is taken from James B. Boles, *Religion in Antebellum Kentucky*, p. 21.

God to revive his work." For the next two years McGready tirelessly preached and prayed with steady, but not spectacular, results.

But a service in July 1799 at the Red River Church saw a religious zeal new to Logan County, and at a similar meeting a month later at Gasper River, a small revival developed so suddenly that even McGready was surprised. Dozens of churchgoers literally fell deathlike to the floor, overcome with their convictions of sin and their belief that the wages of sin was death. Word quickly spread and interest leaped as the sincere and curious alike began to attend the meetings in greater number.

The first truly extraordinary demonstration of religious fervor came in June 1800. That month, several hundred of the most devout members of McGready's three churches gathered at the Red River meetinghouse for a communion service; McGready was assisted by two colleagues, the Reverends William Hodge and John Rankin. The first three days of the four-day meeting were completely normal, but Monday was different. Two new ministers, the brothers John and William McGee, on their way to Ohio had stopped at the services, and, because William had been a convert of McGready in North Carolina, the two were asked to join the preaching even though John was a Methodist. William Hodge preached on Sunday, and suddenly in the middle of his sermon a woman began shouting and singing, then stopped as suddenly as she had begun. Hodge concluded his sermon, and he, McGready, and Rankin prepared to leave the church. The two McGee brothers stayed on, and so did the congregation.

William, filled with excitement, stood up to speak but was overcome with emotion and sat on the floor, weeping. The congregation, now on edge and beginning to sob, waited, not knowing what to expect next. John, the Methodist who had experience in stroking the fires of religious zeal and emotion, rose and with tremulous fervor began to exhort the crowd, telling them that the Holy Spirit was present. The congregation, their nerves tingling at this suggestion that God in his miracle-working power was in their midst, broke out into cries and shouts. McGready, Hodge, and Rankin stood aghast, but decided to let McGee continue his preaching. McGee in turn went down the aisle shouting, exhorting with great loudness and excitement, and immediately the congregation caught the religious fever, falling to the floor in a state of semi consciousness. When the services ended, the ministers concluded they had just witnessed a miraculous visitation of the Holy Spirit.

News spread rapidly, and McGready immediately scheduled another meeting to be held at the Gasper River Church. The services began on Friday of the last weekend of July 1800. Unprecedented crowds gathered, many prepared to stay as long as the meeting continued. On Saturday night, the culmination of two days of preaching bore fruit: two women began shouting. Soon the floor was covered with motionless penitents, convicted of sin and praying for forgiveness.

Nothing similar to the revival meetings in Logan County had ever been seen before in Kentucky. News of them soon spread far and wide. Those who attended went home and spread the word, and soon there was a chain-reaction of similar revivals, sweeping first across Kentucky and then across the entire South.

Barton W. Stone and the Cane Ridge Revival

A similar revival took place, soon after, in and around Cane Ridge, Kentucky (east of Lexington), where in August of 1801 an estimated crowd of from 25,000 to 30,000 people attended a protracted meeting.

Barton W. Stone, a Presbyterian preacher who had accepted the churches at Concord and Cane Ridge in the fall of 1798 through the Presbytery of Transylvania, tells of the apathy in religion in the early 1800's, and of the great revival he witnessed in attending the meetings in Logan County and of his own revival at Cane Ridge, shortly thereafter.

> Things moved on quietly in my congregations, and in the country generally. Apathy in religious societies appeared everywhere to an alarming degree. Not only the power of religion had disappeared, but also the very form of it was waning fast away, and continued so till the beginning of the present century [1800]. Having heard of a remarkable religious excitement in the south of Kentucky, and in Tennessee, under the labors of James McGready and other Presbyterian ministers, I was very anxious to be among them; and, early in the spring of 1801, went there to attend a camp-meeting. There, on the edge of a prairie in Logan County, Kentucky, the multitudes came together, and continued a number of days and nights encamped on the ground; during which time worship was carried on in some part of the encampment. The

scene to me was new, and passing strange. It baffled description. Many, very many fell down, as men slain in battle, and continued for hours together in an apparently breathless and motionless state - sometimes for a few moments reviving, and exhibiting symptoms of life by a deep groan, or piercing shriek, or by prayer for mercy most fervently uttered. After lying thus for hours, they obtained deliverance. The gloomy cloud, which had covered their faces, seemed gradually and visibly to disappear, and hope in smiles brightened into joy - they would rise shouting deliverance, and then would address the surrounding multitude in language truly eloquent and impressive...

The meeting being closed, I returned with ardent spirits to my congregations. I reached my appointment at Cane Ridge on Lord's-day. Multitudes had collected, anxious to hear the religious news of the meeting I had attended in Logan...

The effects of this meeting through the country were like fire in dry stubble driven by a strong wind. All felt its influence more or less. Soon after, we had a protracted meeting at Concord. The whole country appeared to be in motion to the place, and multitudes of all denominations attended...

On the 2nd of July, 1801, I was married to Elizabeth Campbell, daughter of Col. William Campbell and Tabitha his wife, daughter of Gen. William Russell, of Virginia. My companion was pious, and much engaged in religion. We hurried up from Muhlenberg, where her mother lived, to be in readiness for a great meeting, to commence at Cane Ridge shortly after. This memorable meeting came on Thursday or Friday before the third Lord's-day in August, 1801. The roads were literally crowded with wagons, carriages, horsemen, and footmen, moving to the solemn camp. The sight was affecting. It was judged, by military men on the ground, that there were between twenty and thirty thousand collected. Four or five preachers were frequently speaking at the same time, in different parts of the encampment, without confusion. The Methodist and Baptist preachers aided in the work, and all appeared cordially united in it - of one mind and one soul, and the salvation of sinners seemed to be the great object of all...

To this meeting many had come from Ohio and other distant parts, who returned home and diffused the same spirit in their neighborhoods, and the same works followed. So low had religion sunk, and such carelessness universally had prevailed, that I have thought that nothing common could have arrested the attention of the world; therefore these uncommon agitations were sent for this purpose.[7]

Influence of "Great Revival" upon Mill Creek Church

The influence of the *"Great* Revival" meetings of Logan County, and later at Cane Ridge, affected the Mill Creek Baptist Church in that John Mulkey had personally attended the notable Cane Ridge meeting in 1801.

Mulkey had become acquainted with a young preacher by the name of David Haggard from Renox Creek, near Burkesville, Kentucky. Prior to the Cane Ridge meeting, Haggard had written Mulkey requesting that he ride along and attend the meeting with him, which Mulkey accepted.

Burkesville, Ky.
Aug. 2, 1801

Dear Brother John:
Have just received a letter from Barton Stone. He indicates that in May and June there were more than 8,000 attending three revivals conducted around Lexington. Five thousand attended a May communion appointment at the Concord Church. He expects more at the August 7th meeting at Cane Ridge.

Since Baptists, Methodists, and Presbyterians are preaching, I thought you might like to join me at Burkesville for a trip to Cane Ridge. Let me know if you can come.

Yours in His Service,
David[8]

---

[7] Barton W. Stone, *Biography of Elder Barton Warren Stone*, pp. 34-38.
[8] E. Clayton Gooden, *A Fork in the Road*, p. 77.

But the story of David Haggard doesn't end there. Not only was Haggard responsible for exposing Mulkey to the renewed interest in religion that was sweeping through Kentucky, but he had also personally introduced Mulkey to the growing concerns of the *Restoration Movement.*

David Haggard was the brother of Rice Haggard. Both had been Methodist preachers, but had recently left that body and formed a church at Renox Creek that went by the name *"Christians"* only.

Rice, a Methodist circuit-rider, found himself aligned with James O'Kelly - another Methodist preacher - when a group withdrew themselves from that organization during the General Conference which met in Baltimore on November 1, 1792; Haggard, O'Kelly, and others charging that the Methodist government was misusing episcopal powers.[9]

Taking, first, the name "Republic Methodists," the group later determined to lay aside every manuscript and go by the Bible alone; Rice Haggard addressing the group on August 4, 1794, holding forth his Bible and proclaiming:

> Brethren, this is a sufficient rule of faith and practice. By it we are told that the disciples were called Christians, and I move that henceforth and forever the followers of Christ be known as Christians simply.[10]

As a result, in 1801 the "Republic Methodists" changed their name to the Christian Church.

In late June, 1804 Rice Haggard's name is mentioned in conjunction with Barton W. Stone of Kentucky. In 1799 Stone and four other Presbyterian preachers withdrew from the Washington Presbytery after they were charged with heresy for teaching the universality of the gospel and faith as a condition of salvation, and formed the "Springfield Presbytery."[11] But within a year, the group prepared the *"Last Will & Testament of the Springfield Presbytery,"* Stone noting:

---

[9] Earl Irving West, *The Search for the Ancient Order*, Vol. 1, pp. 6-10.

[10] *Ibid*, Vol. 1, p. 10.

[11] Barton W. Stone, *Biography of Elder Barton Warren Stone*, pp. 44-50.

...With the man-made creeds we threw it overboard, and took the name Christian - the name given to the disciples by divine appointment first at Antioch. We published a pamphlet on this name, written by Elder Rice Haggard, who had lately united with us.[12]

A few years later, Barton W. Stone revealed the attitude of these early religious *Restorationists* when he noted:

...It is universally acknowledged, by the various sects of Christians, that the religion of Heaven, for centuries past, has fallen far below the excellency and glory of primitive Christianity. The man, who honestly investigates the cause of this declension, and points the proper way of reformation, must certainly be engaged in a work, pleasing to God, and profitable to man.[13]

Stone went on to establish five principles upon which such a religious restoration could only be accomplished:

1) We must be fully persuaded, that all uninspired men are fallible, and therefore liable to err...

2) We must possess the mind of the honest [John the] Baptist, to be willing to decrease, that Christ may increase - to be willing for truth's sake, to be rejected by all, even to be excluded from the society, with which we may be associated, however popular and respectable it may be...

3) We must be willing to give up all worldly gain or wealth, for the sake of truth...

4) We must learn "to cease from man, whose breath is in his nostrils" - from man, however pious, learned and great he may be accounted. They are all fallible...

---

[12] Barton W. Stone, *Biography of Elder Barton Warren Stone*, p. 50.
[13] Barton W. Stone, *Christian Messenger*, Vol. 1, No. 1, (November 25, 1826), p. 1.

5) We must believe that the Bible was addressed to rational creatures, and designed by God to be understood for their profit.[14]

We make note of all this to show the thinking and attitude of those individuals that John Mulkey came in contact with when he attended the Cane Ridge Revival with David Haggard in late August of 1801. Not only had Mulkey been exposed to the *Great Revival,* he had also come face to face with some Biblical principles that were destined to turn the religious world upside down.

Little did John Mulkey know when he left on his journey to Cane Ridge, that his Baptist principles would be so challenged. It's also doubtful that he could have known at that time that he would soon take a leading role in the attempt to restore New Testament Christianity to a divided religious world.

---

[14] Barton W. Stone, *Christian Messenger*, Vol. 1, No. 1, (November 25, 1826), pp. 2-5.

"I have considered the days of old, the years of ancient times."

Psalms 77:5

A History of the Mill Creek ("Old Mulkey") Church
Tompkinsville, Kentucky

Chapter 2

Formation of the Mill Creek Baptist Church

Monroe County was not created until 1820, being formed from the western portion of Cumberland County and almost the entire eastern portion of Barren County. When the Mulkeys first came to the Mill Creek Settlement - sometime after September 30, 1797 (the Big Pigeon Church Minutes dismissing them by letter), and September 11, 1798 (the earliest known Mill Creek Baptist Church Minutes) - it was located within the boundaries of Barren County.

Cumberland and Barren counties had come into existence in 1798; Cumberland being formed from a portion of Green County, Barren from a portion of Warren County.

By 1798 the military land claims of the Virginia soldiers had been - for the most part - completed, and opened the door for the rush by settlers clamoring for lands not taken south of the Green River by those military claims.[1]

---

[1] *History of the Fitzgeralds and Geralds*, introduction.

It was probably during the ensuing land rush of this year (1798) that the Mulkeys came to the Mill Creek settlement.

That move is recorded in the historical records of the Baptists as follows:[2]

> On September 30, 1797 the following entry was made in the records: (Big Pigeon Baptist Church, Cocke County, Tennessee)
>
> Dismissed, Jno. Mcqueary and wife, Crock Job & wife, Philip Mulkey and wife, Jane Odell, Mark Mitchel and wife, Tho. Sullivan and John Mulkey and sd Mulkey ordered to write letters of dismission [sic] for the above named members."

Others such as David Jobe's family and Abraham Hestand's family obtained letters of dismission on September 1, 1798 and March 30, 1798 respectively.

This small band of pioneer Baptists traveled from the mountains of East Tennessee and settled in the region of the Upper Cumberland Valley, that was to later become Monroe County, Kentucky. Sometime between September 30, 1797 and September 11, 1798, they, along with other Baptists in that locality, formed Mill Creek Baptist Church, better known as "Old Mulkey." They brought with them the old covenant from Big Pigeon Church and inserted it in front of their record book. The first entry in the minutes is dated "Sept. 11, 1798." Mill Creek was a charter member in the formation of the Green River Association in June 1800, at the Beaver Creek Meeting House in Barren County, at which time they helped draft the articles of faith that would be used by over one hundred pioneer Baptist Churches in the central part of Kentucky and Tennessee. These churches located in Barren, Cumberland, Green and Nolin River areas of the aforementioned

---

[2] *Pioneer Baptist Church Records of South-Central Kentucky and the Upper Cumberland of Tennessee 1799-1899*, p. 422.

states, represent some of the oldest churches west of the Allegheny Mountains.[3]

Such a move over great distances was not all that uncommon at that time. The desire for a good piece of land that could support a family was certainly one of the driving forces behind such a difficult move, but bear in mind, also, that these were dedicated Baptists. These pioneer preachers, along with their families, felt that it was their God-given duty to spread the word, regardless of the hardships that might stand in their way.

Modern Baptist historians describe the manner in which the pioneer churches spread, thus:

> The early Baptists utilized the church as a proper agency for promoting the spread of the gospel. The method in carrying out the great commission of our Lord, and one that was a dominant aspect that prevailed in the oldest Baptist churches in the backwoods, was to extend "arms" or "branches" of the mother church into the surrounding country.
> The pastor of the mother church, assisted by several members and licentiates, would attend meetings at the arms, baptizing new converts, and supplying them with preaching. Often the minister had his appointments laid out so as to fill up every Saturday in each month...
> In 1787, the ministers of Buffaloe Ridge church did the ground work which issued in the organization of the Big Pigeon Baptist Church in what is now Cocke County, Tennessee.
> In September 1797, under the leadership of Rev. John Mulkey, several members of Big Pigeon Church removed from Tennessee to what is now Monroe County, Kentucky and organized Mill Creek Baptist Church, the first religious body of any kind in that county...

---

[3] Severn's Valley Church of Hardin County is the oldest church constituted on Kentucky soil (June 18, 1781), and was a member of the Green River Association from 1801 until 1804.

The old mother church at Mill Creek, began at once to send out arms into the territory along the Upper Cumberland River...

After continuing in this manner for a period of time, the arm would usually request for an independent constitution.[4]

How the Mulkeys came to be in East Tennessee was a similar attempt of the early pioneer Baptists to spread the gospel. This story is related in an article by E. Clayton Gooden:

The story of John Mulkey (spelled Mulka by several of his early ancestors) began in Connecticut during the time of the revival preached by George Whitefield (1739-1743).

Whitefield had baptized a young man by the name of Shubeal Stearns, who was later ordained in Tolland, Conn, in 1751. Sterns left Connecticut for the southern part of the colonies, and finally made his home at Sandy Creek, N.C. on November 14, 1755. It was Shubeal Sterns who baptized John Mulkey's grandfather Phillip. Phillip became an ordained minister of the Baptist Church, serving the Deep River congregation from 1759-1760. Later Phillip Mulkey moved to South Carolina where he organized the Broad River Baptist Church. Phillip's son Jonathan, also a Baptist minister, was one of the first resident pastors of Tennessee. Jonathan, who had married Nancy Howard, was preaching in South Carolina when John was born January 14, 1773.[5]

John Mulkey's father, Jonathan, is said to be among the first Baptists to move to Tennessee. Pioneer Baptist historian David Benedict revealed the following:[6]

---

[4] *Pioneer Baptist Church Records of South-Central Kentucky and the Upper Cumberland of Tennessee 1799-1899*, pp. 24-28.

[5] E. Clayton Gooden, January, 1965 issue of the *Discipliana*, reprinted in The Kentucky Explorer, February, 1993, p. 25.

[6] *Pioneer Baptist Church Records of South-Central Kentucky and the Upper Cumberland of Tennessee 1799-1899*, p. 421.

Pioneer Baptist historian Benedict, noted in 1813, that the first Baptists to come to Tennessee: *"there was a small body which went out in something like a church capacity. They removed from the old church at Sandy-Creek, in North Carolina, which was planted by Shubeal Stems; and as a branch of the mother church, they migrated to the wilderness and settled on Boon's Creek. The church is now called Buffaloe Ridge and is under the pastoral care of Jonathan Mulkey."* This same Jonathan Mulkey, who, in 1802, appeared at the Green River Association with a letter of correspondence from the Holston Association.[7]

It was Jonathan Mulkey along with William Reno who did the groundwork which issued in the organization of Big Pigeon Baptist Church in what is now Cocke County, Tennessee. Both Mulkey and Reno continued to visit the settlements of French Broad and Big Pigeon Rivers until a Baptist church could be constituted. On December 6, 1787 the Big Pigeon Baptist Church was organized on the following principles:

We the Members of the Baptist laity on Big Pigeon River being constituted on the principles contained in the Baptist Confession of faith adopted at Philadelphia September the 25th 1742 - do with the full and free consent of our minds give up ourselves to each other and to act in all the decepline [sic] and ordinances of the gospel as a Church of Jesus Christ in witness whereof we have here unto set our names:

Constituted by Isaac Barton & Wilm. Reno
Wilm. Whiteson, David Job, Abram McKay, Elize..th [sic] Whiteson, Serean Job, Rachel McKay, Mourning Prier, Mourning Denton, Darcus Job, Mary White.

---

[7] Benedict, *A History of the Baptist Denomination in America*, Vol. 2, pp. 214-215, also Green River Association, 1802 minutes. Jonathan Mulkey at this same session was also appointed to preach to the congregation on Sunday along with Lewis Moore, Baldwin Clifton, and Elijah Summers.

Received the same day by experience James English and Nickless Wood, Sin [sic].

The constitution now being in its infancy and no meeting hour or particular place of worship we assembled or met at houses convenient in the neighborhood both for Public Worship and for Church business. The Indians soon after breaking out and being troublesome so that we were obliged to be confined to forts which rendered us incapable of conducting our business in a regular manner..."[8]

Early Minutes of Mill Creek Baptist Church

The earliest known entry in the Mill Creek Baptist Church Minute Book is dated September 11th, 1798.

Church met at Harlans and after divine worship proceeded to business as follows:
1st - John and Nancy Compton joined by letter and Bartholomew Wood by living testimony.
2nd - Petitioned for helps to ordain church officers to attend next meeting.
3rd - Jno. Mulkey and John Wood chosen delegates to the asson. [association].
4th - Adjourned till next meeting in course.[9]

In the first article it is noted, *"Church met at Harlans and after divine worship proceeded to business as follows. . ."* From the list of the names of the members in the front of the church book it can be determined that this meeting took place in the home of Samuel Harlan. The early Mill Creek Baptist Church membership list records the names of only three Harlans: Samuel, James, and his wife Eda. However, James and Eda Harlan did not

---

[8] *Minutes of Big Pigeon Baptist Church, 1787-1874*, Cocke County, Tennessee, pp. 1-2.
[9] *Minutes of the Mill Creek Baptist Church*, (September 11, 1798), p. 8

join Mill Creek by letter until March 8, 1800, as recorded in the church's Minute Book.[10]

In the opening article of the next month's meeting, October 13, 1798, the record says, *"Church met at the meeting house..."*, therefore, it can be assumed that the church erected their first permanent meeting house sometime between September 11 and October 13 of the year 1798.

The Association mentioned in the fourth article of business was the old Mero District Association. Prior to the organization of the Green River Association, the Mero District Association - which is another name for the territory along the Cumberland River now known as Middle Tennessee - was the closest available Baptist Association, and the new congregations that sprang up in Central Kentucky at this time, united with this Association.

The Mero District Association was the oldest in that part of the state. It later dissolved, many of its churches uniting with the Green River Association.

John Mulkey, who had been ordained to the ministry by the Holston Association prior to 1796,[11] and John Wood, who was appointed the first elder of the Mill Creek Baptist Church,[12] were chosen as delegates to attend the Mero Association's 1798 annual meeting from the Mill Creek Church.

At the Mill Creek Church's next monthly meeting, October 13, 1798, the minutes of the Mero Association's annual meeting were read and agreed upon.

To further emphasize just how early that the Mill Creek Baptist Church came into existence, in what was then known as Barren County, we see from the early church minutes, as well as from original Barren County Court Records, that John Mulkey was the first United Baptist preacher licensed in the county to perform marriages, as the following entries show:

---

[10] *Minutes of the Mill Creek Baptist Church*, (March 8, 1800), p. 14.

[11] *Pioneer Baptist Church Records of South-Central Kentucky and the Upper Cumberland of Tennessee 1799-1899*, p. 423.

[12] *Minutes of the Mill Creek Baptist Church*, (January 12, 1799), p. 10.

...2. the church grant a certificate to Brother Jno Mulkey in order for him to obtain License to mary [sic]...[13]

The granting of that license was recorded in the first Barren County Court Book as follows:

On Motion of John Mulkey Licence [sic] is granted him to Solemnize the rites of Marriage agreeable to Law he having produced credentials of his Ordination and of his being in regular communion with the United Baptist Church and made oath.[14]

In addition to John Wood being appointed the first elder of the Mill Creek Church (as noted above) Philip Mulkey, John's brother, was appointed the church's first deacon.

...2nd after some examination, the church agrees to appoint and set forward Philip Mulkey to the work of deacon.
3rd concluded that the members are to appropriate money to be lodged in the deacon's hand for the use of the church.[15]

The first act of discipline that is recorded among the Mill Creek Baptist Church begins in March of 1799 when it is noted that one of its members was charged with drunkenness:

March 9, 1799 - ...A complaint laid against Brother Enoch Job for being intoxicated with liquor and he is suspended from privelige, [sic] and Thos Sulivant and Philip Mulkey appointed to cite him to next church meeting.[16]

The records go on to show that Enoch Job did not attend the meeting of the church on April 13, 1799, or the May 11, 1799 meeting. But the church

---

[13] *Minutes of the Mill Creek Baptist Church,* (May 11, 1799), p. 12.
[14] *Court Order Book No. 1, Barren County, Kentucky 1799-1802,* p. 2.
[15] *Minutes of the Mill Creek Baptist Church,* (October 15, 1798), p. 9.
[16] *Ibid,* (March 9, 1799), p. 10.

exercised patience, and as a result, Job did attend the June meeting and was restored:

> June 8, 1799 - Brother Enoch Job came forward and satisfaction being gained he was restored.[17]

Notes concerning when the church would observe communion (the Lord's Supper), and also the time set for the meeting of the church were revealed in the April 1799 minutes:

> April 13, 1799 - 2nd the church agree to commune 3 times in the year, May, July & October.
> 3rd the church agree to meet stated on church meeting days at eleven o'clock and also to have preaching before the church sits to do business...[18]

A controversy came up in March of 1800 concerning the Lord's Day, where the minutes reveal:

> ...2nd the church considered of the Lord's day & thought a reformation necessary among her members & several of them to be worthy of censure, such as Hunting for game, Horse or cow hunting, to save other time cutting fire wood when it could have been procurd [sic] before hand, or any other thing that may not be considered a work of Necessaty [sic] or Mercy.[19]

However, the dispute was resolved as the reading in the left margin of the minute book notes, *"this article of the sabbath dissolved by mutual agreement."*

From these few minutes we are able to see that the early members of the Mill Creek Baptist Church were dedicated men, and even in the wilderness

---

[17] *Minutes of the Mill Creek Baptist Church*, (June 8, 1799), p. 12.
[18] *Ibid*, (April 13, 1799), p. 11.
[19] *Ibid*, (March 8, 1800), pp. 14-15.

of Southern Kentucky, it was their desire to go about their business in an orderly fashion, and in accordance with the Baptist belief.

However, it is also noted that they were patient men who truly loved one another and sought the well-being of each member. There was also an early spirit of liberty exhibited in the ruling concerning the article relating to work that should and should not be done on the Lord's Day.

Overall, their attitude is well summed up in a phrase that appeared in many Baptist documents during this period, which said [translated from Latin]:

> "In essentials unity;
> In nonessentials liberty;
> in all things charity." [20]

The Baptist Associations

At the beginning of the year 1800, it was almost without exception that all Baptist Churches would unite with the closest Baptist Association.

As already noted, when the Mill Creek Baptist Church was formed in Barren County, they aligned themselves with the Mero District Baptist Association of the Middle Tennessee area, that being the Association nearest them at that time.

As the number of churches grew in Southern Kentucky, it was deemed necessary that an Association be formed closer to home. The Mill Creek Church would be one of the charter churches of that body; helping in the subsequent formation of the Green River Association.

Formation of the Green River Association

---

[20] Earl Irving West, *The Search for the Ancient Order*, Vol. 1, p.49.

[21]The Green River Association was the sixth organization of its kind constituted in Kentucky.

In 1799, a conference was held in June at Sinking Creek meetinghouse, in Warren County, for the purpose of considering the propriety of forming a new Baptist Association to serve Southern Kentucky. The conclusion of that meeting was that it was expedient for the churches to associate.

Nothing is noted in the Mill Creek minutes concerning the conference, and the July 1799 minutes of the church were all lost [according to notes in the Mill Creek Minute Book], as were those of August, September, and October of that same year. However, from other documents we know that Mill Creek was one of at least four churches that participated in that preliminary meeting at Sinking Creek. The four churches that we know that participated were:

Dripping Springs Church (Sinks of Beaver Creek), in what is now Metcalfe County, was the oldest of the four congregations to attend the June 1799 meeting, having been constituted February 3, 1798. Delegates sent to this first conference from Dripping Springs were Robert Smith and William Nevill.[22]

Mill Creek Baptist Church was the second oldest church in the area to attend the June 1799 organizational conference, probably because John Mulkey was acting as moderator for the Dripping Springs Church when their delegates were selected.[23]

Mt. Tabor Baptist Church (Beaver Creek) was the third oldest church represented, being constituted November 5, 1798, and sent John Baugh and John Murphy as delegates.[24]

---

[21] Most of the following material on the Green River Association has been obtained from J. H. Spencer, *History of Kentucky Baptist*, Vol. 1. p. 105-ff; and Cawthorn, Warnell, *Pioneer Baptist Church Records of South-Central Kentucky and the Upper Cumberland of Tennessee 1799-1899*, p. 66-ff.

[22] *Minutes of the Mt. Tabor Baptist Church*, (May 1799 entry).

[23] *Minutes of the Dripping Springs Baptist Church*, (May 1799 entry).

[24] *Minutes of the Mt. Tabor Baptist Church*, (May 1799 entry).

Sinking Creek Baptist Church was where the meeting was taking place, this church having been formed in 1798; sometime after November 5 of that year.

The conclusion of the June 1799 meeting was noted in the minutes of the Mt. Tabor Church:

> The conference agree to associate together and appointed the 3rd in Oct. next to meet for that purpose at Beaver Meeting House.[25]

The time and place of the meeting were later changed. Accordingly, messengers from at least nine churches met at Mt. Tabor meetinghouse, in Barren County, on the third Saturday of June 1800 and the constitution of the Green River Association was drafted.

Those minutes of the Mill Creek Church are available, and read:

> ...[the church] appointed brethren John Mulkey, Benjamin Gist, John Wood and Thomas Sulivant to attend an association held on Little barran [sic] the 1st Saturday in November 1800.[26]

Other churches attending this conference were Dripping Springs, Mt. Tabor, Trammel's Fork of Drakes Creek, Trammel's Creek in Green County, Brush Creek, Sinking Creek, Pitman's and Robinson's Creek, and Barren (Blue Springs).

On Saturday, November 1, 1800, the Green River Association met at the Trammel's Creek Meeting House in Green County, and Carter Tarrent was appointed to print the constitution of the Association which had been adopted at the previous session.

The third annual conference of the Green River Association was held at the Mill Creek Church on July 31, 1802.

---

[25] *Minutes of the Mt. Tabor Baptist Church*, (June 1799 entry).

[26] *Minutes of the Mill Creek Baptist Church*, (September, 2nd Saturday, 1800), p. 20.

...Appointed brethren John Mulkey, Benjamin Gist and Obadiah Howard to attend the association at this place last Saturday in July 1802.[27]

The growth of the Green River Association is clearly indicated, in that, at the annual meeting at Mill Creek in 1802, messengers from 30 different churches were present, reporting a combined membership of 1,763, which showed that the numerical strength of the Association had multiplied more than five-fold in two years.[28]

Seeing that questions would come up in the future among the membership of the Mill Creek Baptist Church concerning the authority of Associations, as well as certain issues relating to the Articles of Faith, as a matter of reference, the eleven *Articles of Faith of the Green River Association* are included below:

Articles of Faith of the Green River Association
Adopted at her constitution at the Sinking Creek Meeting House, Warren County, Kentucky, June 1800

Article 1
We believe in one only True and Living God, and that there are a trinity of persons in the God Head, the Father, Son, and Holy Ghost, and yet that there are not three Gods, but one God.

Article 2
We believe that the scripture of the Old and New Testaments are the word of God, and the only rule of faith and practice.

Article 3

---

[27] *Minutes of the Mill Creek Baptist Church,* (June, 1st Saturday, 1802), p. 35.
[28] Frank M. Masters, *A History of Baptists in Kentucky,* p. 70.

We believe in the fall of Adam, and the imputation of his sin to his posterity, the corruption of human nature, and the impotency of man to recover himself by his own free will ability.

Article 4
We believe that sinners are justified in the sight of God only by the righteousness of Christ imputed to them, and that good works are the fruit of faith, and follow after justification, and only justify us in the sight of men and angels, and are evidences of our gracious state.

Article 5
We believe that the saints shall persevere in Grace, and that not one of them shall finally be lost.

Article 6
We believe that there will be a resurrection of the dead and a general or universal judgment, and that the happiness of the righteous and the punishment of the wicked will be eternal.

(Respecting the Gospel Order)
Article 7
We believe that the visible Church of Christ is a congregation of faithful persons, who have obtained fellowship with each other and have given themselves up to the Lord and one another, having agreed to keep up a Godly discipline according to the rules of the Gospel.

Article 8
We believe that Jesus Christ is the great Head of the Church, and that the government thereof is with the body.

Article 9
We believe that water baptism and the Lord's Supper are ordinances of the Lord, and to be continued by his church til [sic] His second coming.

Article 10
We believe that true believers are the only subject of baptism, and that dipping is the only mode.

Article 11
We believe that none but regularly baptized church members have a right to commune at the Lords Table.[29]

* * *

The rapid growth of the Green River Association soon made it profitable that the body divide itself into three separate Associations in order that the churches might be served in a more local capacity.

Division of the Green River Association

On Monday, July 30, 1804, the Green River Association resolved to divide her territory into three parts, each to be a separate Association. This resulted in the formation of two new Associations; Russell Creek and Stockton Valley. The proposed boundary lines were as follows:

> ...beginning at the mouth of Big Barren, thence up Green river to the mouth of Little Barren, thence up Little Barren to the ridge, thence along the ridge each way... Agreed that that part south of Little Barren retain the name Green River Association,... that part north of Little Barren be known by the name Russell's Creek Association... And that part lying east of the Ridge be known by the name Stocktons Valley Association.[30]

---

[29] *Pioneer Baptist Church Records of South-Central Kentucky and the Upper Cumberland of Tennessee 1799-1899*, p. 13; (Copied from the 1800 minutes of the Green River Association at the Liberty of the Southern Baptist Theological Seminary, Louisville, Ky. These 11 Articles of Faith also appear in the records of three of the oldest churches in South-Central Kentucky: Mill Creek Baptist Church, Monroe County; Clear Fork Baptist Church, Clinton County; Casey's Fork Baptist Church, Cumberland County.)

[30] *Minutes of the Green River Association*, 1804 minutes; see also, *Pioneer Baptist Church Records of South-Central Kentucky and the Upper Cumberland of Tennessee 1799-1899*, p. 419.

The Mill Creek Church fell within the boundary of the Stockton Valley Association.

The constitution of the Stockton Valley Association was adopted at the Clear Fort Meeting House in Clinton County in 1805, where they took the same 11 Articles of Faith that had been adopted by the Green River Association.

This meeting was a year after the Green River Association divided its body into three groups. The first meeting of the Stockton Valley Association was apparently put off because the churches that made up this Association were scattered over a very large territory, cut off by large rapid streams and rugged mountains. The records of this first meeting (1805) have been lost, but the minutes of 1806 are preserved, and speak of the preceding year (1805) as *"our first Association."*[31]

Churches represented at the 1806 meeting were Sinking Spring, in Fentress County, Tennessee; Clear Fork (formally Stockton Valley) in Clinton County, Kentucky; Otter Creek and Beaver Creek in Wayne County, Kentucky; Brimstone (gathered by Philip Mulkey as the first *"arm"* of the Mill Creek Church in Clay County, Tennessee); Roaring River and West Fork in Overton County, Tennessee; Cumberland River, Mill Creek, and Mashecks Creek (formally known as Wards Branch, and later as Words Run, the second *"arm"* of the Mill Creek Church)[32] in Monroe County, Kentucky; Caseys Creek in Cumberland County, Kentucky; and Blackburns Fork (location unknown), Salt Lick (location unknown) and Caney Fork (location unknown).

The third session of the Stockton's Valley Association was held at the Mill Creek Church in 1807. Isaac Denton preached the opening sermon. John Mulkey was elected moderator and William Wood the clerk. The 18

---

[31] *Minutes of the Stockton Valley Association*, Page 1 of the Association record book of the minutes affirm that the Association met for conference the first time in 1805.

[32] More concerning the Mill Creek *"arms"* of Brimstone and Wards Branch will be covered in a later chapter.

churches that participated reported that there were 10 baptisms and 806 members that year.[33]

Before we close this chapter relating to the early formation years of the Mill Creek Baptist Church, perhaps it will helpful to the reader that we also include the old covenant of the church.

This church covenant appears in the front of the Mill Creek Church book. It was brought with them to Kentucky when they left the Big Pigeon Baptist Church in Cocke County, Tennessee and appears to have been transcribed in Philip Mulkey's own handwriting.[34]

With some changes in phraseology, the covenant is the same as that of Buffalo Ridge Baptist Church, the oldest remaining Baptist church in the state of Tennessee.[35]

The Old Covenant of Mill Creek Baptist Church

On account of the various opinions now abounding among professors of Christianity concerning covenants or signing we the subscribers believe the practice to be scriptural from the following passages of scripture, viz.: Josh 24:25; II Kings 23:2,3; Neh. 9:28; Jer. 5:5; II Chro. 15:12 - We believe it also to be Necessary duty for the comfort and well being [sic] of us as a church and as such do subscribe the following articles: Holding Believers Baptism by immersion, laying on of hands, particular election or Grace by predestination of God in Christ Jesus, effectual calling by the Holy Ghost, free justification by the imputed righteousness [sic] of Christ, Progressive santification [sic] through God's Grace & truth, and final preservation of the saints in grace, the Resurrection of these our bodies, after death life ever lasting [sic] and Eternal Judgment. We take the only Living & true God

---

[33] Frank M. Masters, *A History of Baptists in Kentucky*, p. 176.

[34] Philip Mulkey was the first clerk of Mill Creek Church. His signature appears on the inside of the front cover of the church record book. After analyzing the handwriting of the old church covenant, it also appears to be in Philip Mulkey's handwriting as well.

[35] *Pioneer Baptist Church Records of South-Central Kentucky and the Upper Cumberland of Tennessee 1799-1899*, p. 422.

to be our God, one God in three persons, the Father, the Son & the Holy Ghost. We take the scriptures of the Old & New Testament to be the revealed mind and will of God and promise through the aid of the Holy Spirit to make them the only rule of our faith & practice & to be governed by it in all church discipline - We do acknowledge ourselves children of wrath by nature & our hope of mercy with God is only through imputed Righteousness of Christ apprehended & received by faith alone. We do promise to bear each other's weakness & infirmities with much tenderness, not discovering them to any out side [sic] the church, But by Gospel order as in Matthew 18:15, 16, 17 & other scripture of the like nature. We believe God acts as a soverign [sic] of all things. Our souls our bodies & all we have is at His soverign [sic] disposal under every act of Providence & in every circumstance of life we should be ready to submit to him as such and do purpose through the aid of Divine Grace so to do believing it will be most for the Glory of God & mutual comfort of each other. We do through the assistance of Divine Grace united by give up ourselves to others as Brethren in Christ. - love to watch over each other in the spirit of meekness guarding against all jesting lightness & foolish talking which is not convenient or any other thing that does not become the followers of the Lamb seeking each other's good in particular the advancement of the Christian religion universally not forsaking the assembling of ourselves together as the manner of some is, but do by filling up our places at the house of God as far as Prividence [sic] shall admit Provoking each other to love & good works submitting ourselves to the government & discipline of this church as a part of Christ's mystical body as we shall be directed by His Word & Spirit.[36]

The phrase pertaining to the *"laying on of hands"* on the newly baptized was dropped by the United Baptist when they constituted the Green River

---

[36] *Minutes of the Mill Creek Baptist Church*, pp. 1-3.

Association, although it was retained by the Holston Association (East Tennessee) for many years.[37]

In conclusion to what has been revealed in this chapter, it is obvious that the Mill Creek Church was not only in good standing with the Baptists in its formative years; it had, from its early constitution, taken a leading role in South-Central Kentucky among the affairs of that religious body.

The same could be said of John and Philip Mulkey. They were obviously judged *"sound in the Baptist faith,"* and as a result, had been elevated to leadership roles within that denomination.

But there were storm clouds gathering that would change all of that.

---

[37] *Pioneer Baptist Church Records of South-Central Kentucky and the Upper Cumberland of Tennessee 1799-1899*, p. 424.

"Remove not the ancient landmark which thy fathers have set."

Proverbs 22:28

A History of the Mill Creek ("Old Mulkey") Church
Tompkinsville, Kentucky

Chapter 3

Religious Storm Clouds Gathering

Since John and Philip Mulkey's names are mentioned in numerous instances in Baptist, and other, documents in connection with Barton W. Stone, it is necessary that the reader become better acquainted with Stone, the religious direction he was pursuing, and his influence upon preachers in Kentucky and other states during the *Restoration Movement*.

References from historians who put the Mulkey's and Stone in the same religious context are many. It is not within the scope of this work to try and list them all, but it will serve to establish the point by listing at least a few.

J. H. Spencer, a noted Baptist historian, went as far as to credit the Stockton Valley Association's excluding of the Brimstone Church - an *"arm"* of the Mill Creek Baptist Church of which Philip Mulkey was the preacher - to the Mulkey's adopting the teachings of Stone.

...About this time [1810], the churches in this Association [Stockton Valley] were much disturbed by the Newlight enthusiasm [for years Stone's group was designated as the "New Light Christian Church", a name of reproach used by that part of the religious world who opposed the *Restoration Movement*.[1]] John and Philip Mulkey, two of the most influential preachers in the Association, were carried away with that fanaticism. Brimstone and Martins Fork churches, together with parties of Middle Ford, Sinking Creek, and Big Spring were excluded from the Association for adopting the Unitarian views and other fanatical sentiments of Barton W. Stone...[2]

C. P. Cawthorn and N. L. Warnell, modern Baptist historians, in no uncertain terms, link the 1809 division of the Mill Creek Baptist Church [as noted in Chapter 1, page 4 of this book] with Mulkey being swayed over to the teaching of Stone.

After a few years, John Mulkey seemed to have adopted the theology of Barton W, Stone. The main point of difference between Stone and the Baptists was over the influence of the death of Christ on God. The Baptists were afraid that Stone and Mulkey's doctrine tended to deism by reducing the death of Jesus to the level of the death of other men. Stone feared that the substitutionary theory of atonement was so contrary to the true nature of Christianity as to be itself a cause of infidelity. He believed that the alternative was the moral influence theory of atonement. The moral influence was exerted on man, and not on God. The death of Christ had a "moral tendency" to lead men to repentance. The other side attempted to expose Mulkey as a deist and an infidel on the question. They were unable to see any merit in the moral influence theory of atonement. To his opponents, Mulkey had reduced the death of Christ to the level of martyrdom.

This doctrine drew a bold challenge from a large percent of the membership [of the Mill Creek Church], who regarded it as a doctrine contrary to the Christian religion, and boldly charged Mulkey with being a heretic. This accusation tormented heated arguments and

---

[1] Earl Irving West, *The Search for the Ancient Order*, Vol. 1, p. 29.
[2] J. H. Spencer, *History of Kentucky Baptist*, Vol. II, p. 214.

unrelenting stands taken by [the] membership. Every effort made to bring about reconciliation of the membership failed...[3]

Even historians among the Disciples of Christ [the name preferred by Alexander Campbell and those associated with him in the *Restoration Movement*.[4]] made a direct link between the Mulkey brothers and Barton W. Stone. In reference to Philip Mulkey removing from Kentucky and Tennessee during the 1830's and establishing *Mulkeytown* in Illinois; along with his sons-in-law John and Robert Kirkpatrick, his daughter Edith, his sons, and other relatives, the following account is related:

> Mr. T.K. (Thomas Kendall) Means was born in Tennessee in April, 1831, and was brought by his parents to Franklin County, Illinois, in 1834. He is still living in Mulkeytown (1915). His mind is vigorous and his thought clear. He says: *"The first settlers of this part of the country called themselves Baptists and met at the house of John Kirkpatrick, who settled here in 1818. But these people had been baptized in Kentucky and Tennessee by John Mulkey and his brother Philip, who were Baptist preachers, but went into the Reformation with Barton W. Stone early in this century. It is a fact that John Mulkey was tried for heresy in 1809 in Kentucky. No one knows when these people left off the name 'Baptists' and adopted the name 'Christians'..."* [5]

There are other references that could be revealed, but these are enough to show that Barton W. Stone was considered a driving force in the *Restoration Movement*, and a man, considered by many, of much influence upon John and Philip Mulkey, as well as upon many other preachers in Kentucky and surrounding states; including ministers from among the Baptists, Methodists, Presbyterians, and others. But in what direction was Barton W. Stone heading?

---

[3] Cawthorn, Warnell, *Pioneer Baptist Church Records of South-Central Kentucky and the Upper Cumberland of Tennessee 1799-1899*, p. 436.

[4] Alexander Campbell, *Millennial Harbinger*, (1830), pp. 372-373.

[5] Nathaniel S. Haynes, *History of the Disciples of Christ in Illinois*, pp. 24-25.

Barton W. Stone

In Chapter 1 of this book, we introduced Barton W. Stone, and told of his being exposed to the *Great Revival* of James McGready in Logan County, Kentucky in 1801. We also noted that, following his attendance at the Logan County revivals, Stone immediately returned to his congregations near Lexington, Kentucky (Concord and Cane Ridge) and scheduled similar revivals; the Cane Ridge Meeting drawing crowds up to an estimated 30,000.

We also noted that David Haggard had requested John Mulkey to accompany him to the Cane Ridge Meeting, Mulkey accepting.

But Stone was a lot more than just the promoter of the Cane Ridge and Concord Revivals.

Stone struck a chord with the Baptists, and other denominations of that day, in several areas. But the two areas that appear most in harmony with those of John and Philip Mulkey, is Stone's conclusions concerning the scope of salvation; and the lack of authority for creeds, confessions of faith, presbyters, councils, associations, and all such man-made bodies, intent upon ruling the affairs of Christians.

The Scope of Salvation

On the subject of the scope of salvation (who could, and who could not, be saved), Stone had come to the conclusion that forgiveness of sins was the *universal* gift of God, and available to all that would accept it. This was in direct opposition to the *Calvinistic* thinking among many of the denominations at that time; that doctrine teaching that only a certain number would, and could, be saved, regardless of their religious state of mind or their attempts toward obedience.

On this subject Stone wrote:

> About this time [just after being called to serve the churches at Cane Ridge and Concord in the fall of 1798] my mind was continually tossed on the waves of speculative divinity, the all-engrossing theme of the

religious community at that period. Clashing, controversial opinions were urged by the different sects with much zeal and bad feeling. No surer sign of the low state of true religion. I at that time believed, and taught, that mankind were so totally depraved that they could do nothing acceptable to God, till his Spirit, by some physical, almighty, and mysterious power had quickened, enlightened, and regenerated the heart, and thus prepared the sinner to believe in Jesus for salvation. I began to plainly see, that if God did not perform this regenerating work in all, it must be because he chose to do it for some, and not for others, and that this depended on His sovereign will and pleasure. It then required no depth of intellect to see that this doctrine is inseparably linked with unconditional election and reprobation, as taught in the Westminster Confession of Faith. They are virtually one; and this was the reason why I admitted the decrees of election and reprobation, having admitted the doctrine of total depravity. They are inseparable.

Scores of objections would continually roll across my mind against this system. These I imputed to be blasphemous suggestions of Satan, and labored to repel them as Satanic temptations, and not honestly to meet them with scriptural arguments. Often when I was addressing the listening multitudes on the doctrine of total depravity, their inability to believe - and of the necessity of the physical power of God to produce faith; and then persuading the helpless to repent and believe the gospel, my zeal in a moment would be chilled at the contradiction. How can they believe? How can they repent? How can they do impossibilities? How can they be guilty in not doing them? Such thoughts would almost stifle utterance, and were as mountains pressing me down to the shades of death. I tried to rest in the common salvo of that day, i.e. the distinction between natural and moral ability and inability. The pulpits were continually ringing with this doctrine; but to my mind it ceased to be relief; for by whatever name it be called, that inability was in the sinner, and therefore he could not believe, nor repent, but must be damned. Wearied with the works and doctrines of men, and distrustful of their influence, I made the Bible my constant companion. I honestly, earnestly, and prayerfully sought for the truth, determined to buy it at the sacrifice of everything else.

On a certain evening, when engaged in secret prayer and reading my Bible, my mind became unusually filled with comfort and peace. I never recollect of having before experienced such an ardent love and tenderness for all mankind, and such a longing desire for their salvation. My mind was chained to this subject, and for some days and nights I was almost continually praying for the ruined world. During this time I expressed my feelings to a pious person, and rashly remarked, so great is my love for sinners, that had I power I would save them all. The person appeared to be horror-stricken, and remarked, Do you love them more than God does? Why then does he not save them? Surely, he has almighty power. I blushed, was confounded and silent, and quickly retired to the silent woods for meditation and prayer. I asked myself, Does God love the world - the whole world? And has he not almighty power to save? If so, all must be saved, for who can resist his power? Had I a friend or child, whom I greatly loved, and saw him at the point of drowning, and utterly unable to help himself, and if I were perfectly able to save him, would I not do it? Would I not contradict my love to him - my very nature, if I did not save him? Should I not do wrong in withholding my power? And will not God save all whom he loves?

These were to me puzzling questions - I could not satisfactorily solve them consistently with my faith. I was firmly convinced, that according to the Scripture, all were not saved - the conclusion then was irresistible, that God did not love all, and therefore it followed of course, that the spirit in me, which loved all the world so vehemently, could not be the Spirit of God, but the spirit of delusion. My mind became involved in gloom, my troubles rolled back upon me with renewed weight, and all my joys were gone. I prostrated myself before God in prayer; but it was immediately suggested, you are praying in unbelief, and *"whatsoever is not of faith is sin."* You must believe or expect no good from the hand of God. But I cannot believe; as soon could I make a world. Then you must be damned, for, *"he that believeth not shall be damned."* - But will the Lord condemn me to eternal punishment for not doing impossibility? So I thought. I shudder while I write it - blasphemy rose in my heart against such a God, and my tongue was tempted to utter it. Sweat profusely burst from the pores of my body, and the fires of hell gat [sic] hold of me. In this uncommon state I remained for two or three days.

From this state of perplexity I was relieved by the precious word of God. From reading and meditating upon it, I became convinced that God did love the whole world, and that the reason why he did not save all, was because of their unbelief; and that the reason why they believed not, was not because God did not exert his physical, almighty power in them to make them believe, but because they neglected and received not his testimony, given in the Word concerning his Son. *"These are written that ye might believe that Jesus is the Christ, the Son of God, and that believing, ye might have life through his name."* I saw that the requirement to believe in the Son of God, was reasonable; because the testimony given was sufficient to produce faith in the sinner; and the invitations and encouragement of the gospel were sufficient, if believed, to lead him to the Saviour, [sic] for the promised Spirit, salvation and eternal life.

This glimpse of faith - of truth, was the first divine ray of light, that ever led my distressed, perplexed mind from the labyrinth of Calvinism and error, in which I had so long been bewildered. It was that which led me into the rich pastures of gospel-liberty. I now saw plainly that it was not against God and Father of our Lord Jesus Christ that I had been tempted to blaspheme, but against the character of a God not revealed in the Scriptures - a character no rational creature can love or honor - a character universally detested when seen even in man; for what man, professing great love for his children, would give them impossible commands, and then severely punish them for not doing them; and all this for his mere good pleasure? What man acting thus would not be despised as a monster, or demon in human shape, and be hissed from all respectable society? Shall we dare to impute such a character to the God of the universe?

Let me here speak when I shall be lying under the clods of the grave. Calvinism is among the heaviest clogs on Christianity in the world. It is a dark mountain between heaven and earth, and is amongst the most discouraging hindrances to sinners from seeking the kingdom of God, and engenders bondage and gloominess to the saints. Its influence is felt throughout the Christian world, where it is least suspected. Its first link is total depravity. Yet are there thousands of precious saints in this system.[6]

But Stone wasn't alone in his thinking. It was the general attitude of many, if not most, of the preachers that were connected with the early revivals in Logan County, Cane Ridge, Concord, and other localities, that the doctrine of *Calvinism* was foreign to the scriptures, and that faith and salvation was the right of all mankind.

Even from among his own religious body (the Presbyterian Church), Stone was associated with other preachers that were headed in the same direction he was.

Of that group of Presbyterian ministers, he writes:

> There were at this time five preachers in the Presbyterian connection, who were in the same strain of preaching, and whose doctrine was different from that taught in the Confession of Faith of that body. Their names were Richard McNemar, John Thompson, John Dunlavy, Robert Marshall, and myself [Barton Stone]; the three former lived in Ohio, the two latter in Kentucky. David Purviance was then a candidate for the ministry, and was of the same faith...
>
> The distinguishing doctrine preached by us was, that God loved the world - the whole world, and sent his Son to save them, on the condition that they believed in him - that the gospel was the means of salvation - but that this means would never be effectual to this end, until believed and obeyed by us - that God required us to believe in his Son, and had given us sufficient evidence in his Word to produce faith in us, if attended to by us - that sinners were capable of understanding and believing the testimony, and of acting upon it by coming to the Saviour [sic] and obeying him, and from him obtaining salvation and

---

[6] Barton W. Stone, *Biography of Elder Barton Warren Stone*, pp. 30-34.

the Holy Spirit. We urged upon the sinner to believe *now*, and receive salvation - that in vain they looked for the Spirit to be given them, while they remained in unbelief - they must believe before the Spirit or salvation would be given them - that God was as willing to save them now, as he ever was, or ever would be - that no previous qualification was required, or necessary in order to believe in Jesus, and come to him - that if they were sinners, this was their divine warrant to believe in him, and to come to him for salvation - that Jesus died for all, and that all things were now ready. When we began first to preach these things, the people appeared as just awakened from the sleep of ages - they seemed to see for the first time that they were reasonable beings, and that a refusal to use the means appointed, was a damning sin...[7]

Ironically, it was this attitude toward the universal scope of salvation that actually led to the consideration of our next subject; that being the scriptural authority of creeds, confessions of faith, associations, etc.

The Authority Question

It is interesting, indeed, to see the progression that unfolded as the principles of the *Restoration Movement* began to be taught at the turn of the 1800's.

However, we should not be surprised to see, that as one unscriptural position was challenged and shown to be foreign to the Bible, that, of necessity, other false premises that authorized and supported that principle, would begin to naturally tumble as well.

So it was with the authority question.

The doctrine of *Calvinism* denied the universal scope of salvation as taught in the scriptures. Therefore, when Stone and others began to preach that Biblical principle; that God loved the *whole* world and that it was God's desire that *all* should be saved, the very foundation of *Calvinism* was challenged and brought to the forefront. However, not only was the doctrine

---

[7] Barton W. Stone, *Biography of Elder Barton Warren Stone*, pp. 44-45.

brought into question, but the collective bodies that supported the *Calvinistic* teachings were placed under scrutiny as well.

When Barton Stone, Richard McNemar, John Thompson, John Dunlavy, Robert Marshall, and David Purviance saw that they could not accept the clear teachings of the Bible without coming under fire from the religious organization to which they belonged, serious questions were raised in their minds. Moreover, these men found themselves in a position where they were forced to make a decision.

Immediately following the above quotes from Barton Stone on the scope of salvation, let the reader notice the reaction:

> ...The sticklers for orthodoxy amongst us writhed under these doctrines [the universal appeal of salvation], but seeing their mighty effects on the people, they winked at the supposed errors, and through fear, or other motives, they did not at first publicly oppose us. They plainly saw their Confession of Faith neglected in the daily ministration by the preachers of the revival, and murmured at the neglect. In truth, that book had been gathering dust from the commencement of the excitement, and would have been completely covered from view, had not its friends interposed to prevent it. At first, they were pleased to see Methodists and Baptists so cordially uniting with us in worship, no doubt, hoping they would become Presbyterians. But as soon as they saw these sects drawing away disciples after them, they raised the tocsin of alarm - the confession is in danger! - the church is in danger! O Israel to your tents!
>
> These sticklers began to preach boldly the doctrines of their confession, and used their most potent arguments in their defense. The gauntlet was now thrown, and a fire was now kindled that threatened ruin to the great excitement; it revived the dying spirit of partyism, and gave life and strength to trembling infidels and lifeless professors...
>
> In this state of confusion, the friends of the Confession were indignant at us for preaching doctrines so contrary to it. They determined to arrest our progress and put us down. The Presbytery of Springfield, in Ohio, first took McNemar through their fiery ordeal, for

preaching the anti-calvinistic doctrines. From that Presbytery his case came before the Synod at Lexington, Kentucky. That body appeared generally very hostile to our doctrine, and there was much spirited altercation among them. The other four of us well knew what would be our fate, by the decision on McNemar's case; for it was plainly hinted to us, that we would not be forgotten by the Synod. We waited anxiously for the issue, till we plainly saw it would be adverse to him, and consequently to us all.

In a short recess of Synod, we five withdrew to a private garden, where, after prayer for direction, and a free conversation, with perfect unanimity we drew up a protest against the proceeding of Synod in McNemar's case, and a declaration of our independence, and of our withdrawal from their jurisdiction, but not from their communion...[8]

The reader will notice that the progression was simple; the conclusion a natural series of events.

These Presbyterian preachers let the Bible speak on the subject of salvation, however, it proved to be a principle that the *Presbyterian Confession of Faith* did not sanction, and consequently, could not allow. The Presbytery of Springfield, Ohio and the Synod at Lexington, Kentucky were forced to take action. However, in the midst of that action, these men [Richard McNemar, John Thompson, John Dunlavy, Robert Marshall, Barton Stone, and David Purviance] realized that the very foundation on which these man- made bodies stood upon were also faulty, forcing their withdrawal.

For a time, however, their separation duplicated the unscriptural mistakes of those bodies they were trying to free themselves from, as later noted by Stone himself:

> Immediately after our separation from Synod, we constituted ourselves into a Presbytery, which we called the *Springfield Presbytery*. We wrote a letter to our congregations, informed them of what had transpired, and promised shortly to give them and the world a full account of our views of the gospel, and the causes of our separation

---

[8] Barton W. Stone, *Biography of Elder Barton Warren Stone*, pp. 45-47.

from Synod. This book we soon after published, called *The Apology of Springfield Presbytery*. In this book we stated our objections at length to the *Presbyterian Confession* of Faith, and against all authoritative confessions and creeds formed by fallible men. We expressed our total abandonment of all authoritative creeds, but the Bible alone, as the only rule of our faith and practice... Under the name of Springfield Presbytery we went forward preaching, and constituting churches; but we had not worn our name more than a year, before we saw it savored of a party spirit. With the man-made creeds we threw it overboard, and took the name *Christian* - the name given to the disciples by divine appointment first at Antioch [Acts 11:26]. We published a pamphlet on this name, written by Elder Rice Haggard, who had lately united with us. Having divested ourselves of all party creeds, and party names, and trusting alone in God, and the word of his grace, we became a by-word and laughing stock to the sects around; all prophesying our speedy annihilation. Yet from this period I date the commencement of that reformation, which has progressed to this day...[9]

    Immediately following this action, Stone and those associated with the recently-formed Springfield Presbytery, published a document called *The Last Will and Testament of the Springfield Presbytery*. Their thinking was, if there was no scriptural authority for such organizations as the Synod of Kentucky, what right had they to leave that body and form another, different in name, but based on equally unscriptural grounds. There was only one logical solution: the Springfield Presbytery must be laid to rest.

    Since the average reader will not have access to *The Last Will and Testament of the Springfield Presbytery*, we include it here.[10]

The Last Will and Testament of the Springfield Presbytery

    For where a testament is, there must of necessity be the death of the testator; for a testament is of force after men are dead, otherwise it is of no

---

[9] Barton W. Stone, *Biography of Elder Barton Warren Stone*, pp. 48-49.
[10] *Ibid*, pp. 51-53.

strength at all, while the testator liveth. Thou fool, that which thou sowest is not quickened except it die. Verily, verily I say unto you, except a corn of wheat fall into the ground, and die, it abideth alone; but if it die, it bringeth forth much fruit. Whose voice then shook the earth; but now he hath promised, saying, yet once more I shake not the earth only, but also heaven. And this word, yet once more, signifies the removing of those things that are shaken as of things that are made, that those things which cannot be shaken may remain. - *Scripture.*

LAST WILL AND TESTAMENT, &c.

The Presbytery of Springfield, sitting at Caneridge, in the county of Bourbon, being, through a gracious Providence, in more than ordinary bodily health, growing in strength and size daily; and in perfect soundness and composure of mind; but knowing that it is appointed for all delegated bodies once to die: and considering that the life of every such body is very uncertain, do make, and ordain this our Last Will and Testament, in manner and form following, viz:

Imprimis. We *will,* that this body die, be dissolved, and sink into union with the Body of Christ at large; for there is but one body, and one Spirit, even as we are called in one hope of our calling.

Imprimis. We *will,* that our name of distinction, with its Reverend title, be forgotten, that there be but one Lord over God's heritage, and his name one.

Item. We *will,* that our power of making laws for the government of the church, and executing them by delegated authority, forever cease; that the people may have free course to the Bible, and adopt *the law of the Spirit of life in Christ Jesus.*

Item. We *will,* that candidates for the Gospel ministry henceforth study the Holy Scriptures with fervent prayer, and obtain license from God to preach the simple Gospel, *with the Holy Ghost sent down from Heaven,* without any mixture of philosophy, vain deceit, traditions of men, or the rudiments of the world. And let none henceforth take *this honor to himself, but he that is called of God, as was Aaron.*

Item. We *will,* that the church of Christ resume her native right of internal government - try her candidates for the ministry, as to their soundness in the faith, acquaintance with experimental religion, gravity and aptness to teach; and admit no other proof of their authority but Christ speaking in them. We will, that the church of Christ look up to the Lord of the harvest to send forth laborers into his harvest; and that she resume her primitive right of trying those *who say they are apostles, and are not.*

Item. We *will,* that each particular church, as a body, actuated by the same spirit, choose her own preacher, and support him by free will offering, without a written *call* or *subscription* - admit members - remove offenses; and never henceforth *delegate* her right of government to any man or set of men whatever.

Item. We *will,* that the people henceforth take the Bible as the only sure guide to heaven; and as many as are offended with other books, which stand in competition with it, may cast them into the fire if they choose; for it is better to enter into life having one book, than having many to be cast into hell.

Item. We *will,* that preachers and people, cultivate a spirit of mutual forbearance; pray more and dispute less; and while they behold the signs of the times, look up, and confidently expect that redemption draweth nigh.

Item. We *will,* that our weak brethren, who may have been wishing to make the Presbytery of Springfield their king, and wot not what is now become of it, betake themselves to the Rock of Ages, and follow Jesus for the future.

Item. We *will,* that the Synod of Kentucky examine every member, who may be *suspected* of having departed from the Confession of Faith, and suspend every such suspected heretic immediately; in order that the oppressed may go free, and taste the sweets of gospel liberty.

Item. We *will,* that Ja - -, [sic] the author of two letters lately published in Lexington, be encouraged in his zeal to destroy *partyism.* We will, moreover, that our past conduct be examined into by all who may have correct information; but let foreigners beware of speaking evil things which they know not.

Item. Finally we *will,* that all our *sister bodies* read their Bibles carefully, that they may see their fate there determined, and prepare for death before it is too late.

Springfield Presbytery,
June 28th, 1804.
L.S.

Robert Marshall,
John Dunlavy,
Richard M'Nemar,   <u>Witnesses</u>.
B. W. Stone,
John Thompson,
David Purviance

The Last Will and Testament of the Springfield Presbytery was not something done in a corner. It was a document that soon saw great exposure throughout the religious world, and even today, is one of the classic writings to be preserved from the *Restoration* era.

The document was reprinted in a number of publications, consequently, exhibiting a wide influence for a number of years after its original publication.

Stone even reprinted it several years later in the *Christian Messenger,* after it appeared in a monthly periodical called *"The Christian,"* published in St. John's, New Brunswick, that publication noting that it had *"come to us in 'Benedict's history of the Baptists.'"*[11]

Conclusion

Since Rice Haggard was associated with Barton Stone at this time;[12] and that Rice and his brother David were the leading forces in the establishment of a *"Christian"* church near Burkesville, Kentucky; and that David

---

[11] Barton W. Stone, *Christian Messenger,* (January 1841), Vol. 11, pp. 170-171.

[12] Barton W. Stone, *Biography of Elder Barton Warren Stone,* p. 50.

Haggard and John Mulkey were well acquainted, having attended together the Cane Ridge Revival; it is only natural that we assume that Mulkey was aware of *The Last Will and Testament of the Springfield Presbytery*, and the events leading up to it, as well as the religious reforms which Barton Stone contended.

This view is further supported by noting the similarities between that document of Stone's, and John Mulkey's *A Circular Letter Addressed to the Christian Churches in the Western Country";* [printed by] J. A. Woodson, Glasgow, Ky. 1821.

Look at how Mulkey speaks concerning the doctrine of Calvinism and the scope of salvation:

> ...it is generally well known, that some years ago a dissatisfaction took the doctrine of unconditional Election, and some other subjects; which led to much disputation, and finally terminated in an entire separation of myself and a number of others from the Baptist Church...[13]

And on the subject of creeds and confessions of faith:

> ...After much deliberation and free conversation on every subject that came under our view, we finally concluded that all human creeds and confessions of faith were the works of fallible man and consequently they were imperfect and contradictory to each other and also that they had been the cause of many, if not most of the divisions in the church of God; likewise that they all had their zealous advocates, and, of course were calculated to divide Christians, and keep them apart. And further, believing that Christ is the great head of the church and King of Zion, the only Christian lawgiver, and that he had given a sufficiency of laws, rules and regulations, for the government of his church and people. We proceeded to unite ourselves as a Christian Society, agreeable to our best views of the Gospel; having, as we hoped first given to our Lord - we then gave

---

[13] See *Appendix A* of this book, p. (A-2).

ourselves to each other, by the will of God, to be subject to Christ and to each other in the Gospel, taking the Holy Scriptures as the only rule of our faith and practice, we therefore receive all whom we believe Christ has received, with the exception only of such as have been excluded from other societies, for immoral conduct; in that case we esteem it our duty, first to confess their faith to their brethren whom they offended: but if any are cast off using this religious liberty, we freely receive them, - believing that Christ has made them free, and that liberty of conscience is a right that God has conferred on his intelligent creatures and none has the right to take it from them, seeing that they are to account to God alone, for their religious conduct. Thus we have lived together in peace and brotherly love, generally speaking, and have in no instance found any deficiency in the sacred rule we have adopted, but have reason to thank God and take courage...[14]

But, let not the reader interpret that we are advocating that John Mulkey came to these conclusions simply at the urging of Barton W. Stone, or any other man, or group of men, associated with the *Restoration Movement.*

That they were on common ground is true. That historians note their sharing similar beliefs is also true.

As to the source of those beliefs, however, both men acknowledge that their actions were in response to the revealed Word of God; the New Testament scriptures.

Perhaps Homer Hailey best sums up such unions of thought during the *Restoration Movement*, when he says:

> "...the harmony of views was simply the result of studying the same book, with the same desire to learn and do its bidding and return in all things to the New Testament pattern."[15]

---

[14] See *Appendix A* of this book, pp. (A-3), (A-4).
[15] Homer Hailey, *Attitudes and Consequences in the Restoration Movement*, p. 47.

Coming to those conclusions shaped the future of the churches with which Barton W. Stone was associated.

Those same conclusions also served to map the future direction of the churches with which John and Philip Mulkey labored; an influence that reached well beyond the bounds of just the Mill Creek Baptist Church, as we will see in our next chapter.

A History of the Mill Creek ("Old Mulkey") Church
Tompkinsville, Kentucky

Chapter 4

The Spreading of the Mill Creek Church

Soon after the formation of the Mill Creek Baptist Church, in what would later be known as Monroe County, the church began to spread its bounds throughout the immediate area.

As previously noted in Chapter 2, page 21 of this book, it was the familiar practice of primitive Baptist churches to extend themselves throughout the communities in which they settled. That pioneer practice is described in this manner:

> The early Baptists utilized the church as a proper agency for promoting the spread of the gospel. The method in carrying out the great commission of our Lord, and one that was a dominant aspect that prevailed in the oldest Baptist churches in the backwoods was to extend "arms" or "branches" of the mother church into the surrounding country.
>
> The pastor of the mother church, assisted by several members and licentiates, would attend meetings at the arms, baptizing new converts, and supplying them with preaching. Often the minister had

his appointments laid out so as to fill up every Saturday in each month...[1]

That the Mill Creek Church followed this practice is also recorded:

> The old mother church at Mill Creek began at once to send out arms into the territory along the Upper Cumberland River...
> After continuing in this manner for a period of time, the arm would usually request for an independent constitution...[2]

According to the original minutes of the Mill Creek Baptist Church, the first *"arms"* to be extended took place in 1802.

A total of four references in the 1802 minutes are related to the subject of *"arms,"* those appearing in April, June, July, and November.

However, it is thought by some Baptist Church historians that the first three of those references all relate to one extension; that being the church at Brimstone, the last reference, being extended at Wards Branch.

It appears certain that the first and last references are concerned with two different groups; the first being Brimstone, the second Wards Branch.

As a matter of reference for the reader, the Minutes of the Mill Creek Baptist Church that concern these *"arms"* are included here:

> Saturday, April 10th, 1802 - Brethren Sam'l Denton & Welcome Ussery apply for helps in as order to Inquire In to the fitness of a part of this Church for constitution. The Church agrees to hold Church meeting at A'bram Dentons on the fourth Saturday this month. In order for that business and that John Mulkey, Philip Mulkey, John Wood, and Benjamin Gist are Sent by the Church to that worke [sic]...[3]

---

[1] *Pioneer Baptist Church Records of South-Central Kentucky and the Upper Cumberland of Tennessee 1799-1899*, p. 24.

[2] *Ibid*, p. 28.

[3] *Minutes of the Mill Creek Baptist Church*, (April 10, 1802), p. 33.

Saturday, June 12, 1802 - A letter from a part of this Church on Mill Creek South of Cumberland River for helps in order to Inquire into their fitness for constitution. Agree to answer them next meeting...[4]

Saturday, July 10, 1802 - The Church give up part of the Church South of Cumberland River for constitution if found fit when a presbytery for that purpose is Asurtained [sic]...[5]

November 13, Saturday, 1802 - ...The Members on Wards Branch given up to be constituted an arm of this Church, Sarah Judah and Jas Wright, David Lisaan and Rebekah Jobe and James Cole dismissed...[6]

Brimstone

Baptist historian J. H. Spencer credits Philip Mulkey with forming the Brimstone church:

Philip Mulkey was one of the early preachers of the [Stockton Valley] Association. He appears to have gathered the church, originally called Brimstone, which was a member of Green River Association, from 1802, till the constitution of Stocktons Valley, and was under the care of Mr. Mulkey, from its organization, till 1812...[7]

Brimstone is noted in the Baptist Association records of, first the Green River Association, 1802-1804; then in the Stockton Valley Association, 1806-1808; formally excluded from that Association in 1812.[8]

---

[4] *Minutes of the Mill Creek Baptist Church*, (June 12, 1802), pp. 34-35.
[5] *Ibid*, (July 10, 1802), p. 35.
[6] *Ibid*, (November 13, 1802), p. 39.
[7] J. H. Spencer, *History of Kentucky Baptist*, Vol. II. pp. 217-218.
[8] *Pioneer Baptist Church Records of South-Central Kentucky and the Upper Cumberland of Tennessee 1799-1899*, p. 505.

From that same historical source, the following is noted concerning Brimstone:

> The location of Brimstone Church is thought to have been near the mouth of Brimstone Creek [Clay County, Tennessee] and was later moved to the "Big Bottoms" on the Cumberland River at the old Robert Kirkpatrick farm. The name appears to have been changed in later years to "Old Bethel."
>
> The earliest record of a church on Brimstone Creek is contained in an entry in the Mill Creek Church book April 10,1802 ..." Brethren enquire into the fitness of a part of this church for constitution"..."A door opened for the reception of members three came forward and joined by experience: Peggy Grogg, Elijah Denton, and Abram Denton by recantation."
>
> Three months later Abraham Denton appeared along with Philip Mulkey and Welcome Ussery as messengers to the Green River Association. At that time the church reported a membership of 27.[9]

Records of both the Green River and Stockton Valley Associations record the following information concerning Brimstone:

Green River Association

1802, (Messengers) Philip Mulkey, Aberham Denton, Welcome Ussery, (Members) 27.

1803, (Messengers) Philip Mulkey, Sam'l Denton, James Clark, (Members) 34.

1804, (Messengers) Philip Mulkey, John Denton, James Clark, (Members) 51.

---

[9] *Pioneer Baptist Church Records of South-Central Kentucky and the Upper Cumberland of Tennessee 1799-1899*, p. 502.

Stockton Valley Association

1806, (Messengers) Philip Mulkey, Samuel Denton, J. Denton, (Members) 47.

1807, (Messengers) Philip Mulkey, Wm. Massel, Sam'l Denton, (Members) 44.

1808, (Messengers) Philip Mulkey, B. Denton, (Members) 34.

1812, Formally excluded from the Stockton Valley Association.

Brimstone is mentioned by name in the Mill Creek Church book as early as the second Saturday in October, 1802, when it notes:

> ...A comitee [sic] from this Church to meet Capt. Hamiltons on Mill Creek on the 3rd Friday in December, also that we petition Brimstone Church for helps and that we call for Roaring River Church to authenticate the charge against Bro. Wooden, also call Salem Church in the same...[10]

and again in August, 1803:

> ...Bro. Isaac Means Junr. Set at liberty to exercise his gift within the Bounds of this & [?] Brimstone Church...[11]

Some modern Baptist historians feel that the Mill Creek Church entry of June 12, 1802 might have implications concerning the Brimstone Church, and offer the following support:

> There is a possibility that the members of Brimstone Church met on both sides of the Cumberland River. It was years in some cases before

---

[10] *Minutes of the Mill Creek Baptist Church*, (October, 2nd Saturday, 1802), p. 37.
[11] *Ibid*, (August 13, 1803), p. 43.

the early churches in the wilderness of Kentucky and Tennessee had permanent meeting house. They conducted their services in the homes of various members. The early members of Brimstone had family connections south of the Cumberland River. William Tinsley, born 1735, "was the first white man to cross the Big Hill at Butlers Landing and record the 1000 acre land grant from the government." [12]

William Tinsley and his wife Elizabeth came from Virginia and settled in what is now Metcalfe County, Kentucky. Their son, John Tinsley, was born in Kentucky in 1796. William and Elizabeth joined the Dripping Spring Baptist Church on January 3, 1801. They are last mentioned in the church records in September 1803.[13] Sometime after this they moved to the Tinsley Bottom on the Cumberland River in Clay County, Tennessee, while it was still "a canebrake [sic] and woods."

Welcome Ussery who entered 150 acres of land near Line Creek, November 12, 1798, appears as an early member of Brimstone. Mary Ussery who married Sylvanus Fowler lived on the south side of Cumberland River in the Tinsley Bottoms opposite the mouth of Brimstone Creek. John Tinsley married Alice Mulkey, a daughter of Philip Mulkey, the pastor of Brimstone Church. John and Alice owned land on the south side of Cumberland River. They are buried in the High Ceders Cemetery in the Tinsley Bottoms along with a son of Philip Mulkey.

Land grant 221 dated Feb. 4, 1825 was issued to Philip Mulkey on the south side of the Cumberland River between the farms of Sylvanus Fowler and John Tinsley...[14]

---

[12] Kibbie Gardenhire, *The Memoirs of Kibbie Tinsley Williams Gardenhire,* May 12, 1939, a great-granddaughter of William Tinsley, (from footnotes of *Pioneer Baptist Church Records of South-Central Kentucky and the Upper Cumberland of Tennessee 1799-1899*, p. 613.)

[13] *Minutes of Dripping Spring Baptist Church*, entries for January 3, 1801 and September 1803.

[14] *Pioneer Baptist Church Records of South-Central Kentucky and the Upper Cumberland of Tennessee 1799-1899*, pp. 502-503.

Brimstone was one of 14 churches that were represented when the Stockton Valley was formed out of the larger Green River Association in 1805.[15]

However, as noted above, that Association formally excluded Brimstone from its organization in 1812 for the following reasons:

> About this time the New Lights, the followers of Barton W. Stone, came into the [Stockton Valley] Association. Two preachers [John and Philip Mulkey], two churches [Mill Creek and Brimstone] and members of three other churches went off with Stone, but were all excluded from the Association...[16]

and again,

> ...About this time [1810], the churches in this Association [Stockton Valley] were much disturbed by the Newlight enthusiasm John and Philip Mulkey, two of the most influential preachers in the Association, were carried away with that fanaticism. Brimstone and Martins Fork churches, together with parties of Middle Ford, Sinking Creek, and Big Spring were excluded from the Association for adopting the Unitarian views and other fanatical sentiments of Barton W. Stone...[17]

and again,

> ...Brimstone Church continued to grow in membership until 1804 when it reported a membership of 51 at the Green River Association. It appears at this time that the element of discord was sown, which ultimately led to the exclusion of this church from the Stockton Valley Association. Contained in the 1804 minute of the Green River Association is the following notation: "The request of the churches at Kettle Creek and Brimstone to attend the preaching of Benjamin Lynn,

---

[15] J. H. Spencer, *History of Kentucky Baptist*, Vol. 11. p. 213.

[16] Frank M. Masters, *A History of Baptists in Kentucky*, p. 176.

[17] J. H. Spencer, *History of Kentucky Baptist*, Vol. II, p. 214.

granted" The previous year the Green river Association had "advise(d) the churches in her union to be aware (sic) of Benjamin Lynn that they do not attend to his ministry, or call him to officiate in any part of the ministerial function, as he has departed from the principles of our constitution and regulations of our association." ...

In 1809 when John Mulkey was excluded from Mill Creek Church for falling into "Arianism," Philip Mulkey appeared to have withdrawn from the Stockton Valley Association and joined the "Newlight movement" along with his brother.

At the 1812 Stockton Valley Association it was reported that "Brimstone being disorderly is dropped" and "Philip Mulkey (of Brimstone) is in disorder and excluded from association. This is the last account we have of Brimstone Church...[18]

Wards Branch

Personal research by the author reveals much more about the *"arm"* at Wards Branch than is found in works available by Baptist historians.

Wards Branch is a very small, and short, creek that runs just north of the present-day location of the Sulphur Ridge church of Christ, six and a half miles east of Tompkinsville, Kentucky.

Wards Branch crosses Highway 100 on the land of Virgil Hammer, where it then travels southeast and empties into the Cumberland River.

Early Baptist historical records gave this early *"arm"* at Wards Branch the name of Mashek's Creek Church (later called, Word's Run)[19] where they include the minutes of November 13, 1802 from the *Minutes of the Mill Creek Baptist Church.*

The adoption of the name *Mashek's Creek Church* is probably due to the fact that much of this area in eastern Monroe County was known as *"Mashek,"* as it was one of the first spots to be settled in the county, and

---

[18] *Pioneer Baptist Church Records of South-Central Kentucky and the Upper Cumberland of Tennessee 1799-1899*, pp. 503-504.
[19] *Ibid*, p. 450-451.

later flourished into a dominant community following the land rush of the late 1700's and early 1800's. It included land from what is known today as Old Temple Hill, all the way down to near Center Point where the creek empties into the Cumberland River, a distance of around eight miles.

Moses Kirkpatrick appears to have been the first to settle in this area as early as 1776, although it appears that he had visited the area much sooner.[20]

The creek got its name in honor of an early hunter that was killed there by Indians.

> In the Green County, Kentucky Land Entries, dated July 30, 1796 is the following entry: "James McColgan enters 200 acres of land upon a certificate No. 10 granted by the commissioners lying on the creek MARSHEK SCAGGS was killed on the waters of Cumberland."[21]

When the gospel was first sent to the Green River section of Kentucky, the land was wild and uncultivated. Alas! for the poor Baptists, death at the hands of a lawless savage was an ever present chill on the hearts of the living, and who could tell whether it would continue to advance with the quiet of a blight, or yet burst upon them with the fury of a tempest?

A great number of these first Baptists were among the "Long Hunters" who came from the "Baptist Valley" area of Southwest Virginia.

These families were the forerunners of the "foot-washing" Baptists which subsequently moved into Kentucky and established many of the Baptist Churches of the frontier land. Among the leaders was the Skaggs family consisting of Rev. James Skaggs and his brothers Henry, Richard, Jacob, Charles, Moses, and William. These were the early "Long Hunters" of 1761-1775 of which the Kentucky historians have recorded much about. Henry and Richard were particularly prominent.

---

[20] *History of the Fitzgeralds and Geralds*, ("Original Settlers of Meshack Creek, Blands Fork, and Mud Camp Areas").

[21] *Pioneer Baptist Church Records of South-Central Kentucky and the Upper Cumberland of Tennessee 1799-1899*, p. 450.

Henry Skaggs was at the present site of Bowling Green, Kentucky in 1775. A brother, Moses, was killed by Indians on his second trip to Kentucky.

Richard Skaggs had three sons named Shadrach, Mashack, and Abednego. It was Mashack who was killed by Indians on the creek named after him in present Monroe County, Kentucky.[22]

Had the Mill Creek Church minutes not specifically mentioned *"Wards Branch,"* we might never have known the precise location of this early *"arm"* of the mother church. But they did, therefore, at least this much is certain; the Wards Branch *"arm"* was at what would later be known as the Sulphur Ridge community.

According to those same Baptist historical records the Mashek's Creek (Wards Branch, Words Run) Church made application into the Green River Baptist Association in 1803 and listed a membership of 11 people, including Dennis Pottinger whose family migrated to that area from Pottinger's Station (a fort in central Kentucky) after Cumberland County was formed in 1798, Fleming Smith (Revolutionary War soldier), Thomas Ray who entered land on *"Mashek's Creek"* in 1799, Andrew and David Gimlin, and Charnell Glascock.

Although some of the letters in the last name are not certain, it appears that a William Gimlin obtained a land grant in 1800, which included Wards Branch.[23]

Messengers from Wards Branch, sent to the 1803 Green River Association meeting, were Thomas Ray, Dennis Pottinger, and Charnell Glascock.

David Gimlin and Thomas Ray were the messengers to the Association's 1804 meeting, recording their membership at 14.

In 1805, when the Stockton Valley Association was constituted, the church entered that body.

---

[22] *Pioneer Baptist Church Records of South-Central Kentucky and the Upper Cumberland of Tennessee 1799-1899*, p. 62.

[23] *History of the Fitzgeralds and Geralds*, p. (-a-), also accompanying map.

In that Association's first meeting in 1806, the church sent Fleming Smith and David Gimlin as messengers, their reported membership still being at 14. In the meeting of that Association in 1807, the same two men were sent as messengers, the membership up to 18 at that time.

Following the above Association record of 1807, the name of the church vanished from the list of the Stockton Valley Association.

For those familiar with Baptist Church history in Monroe County, the church at Wards Branch is not to be confused with the Baptist churches that later appeared in the Mashek Creek area as *"arms"* of the Mill Creek Church in the years of 1841 and 1859. These were different churches and had no connection with the original *"arm"* at Wards Branch, as indicated by the following records:

> Bro. Wm. Chism and Bro. Savage be authorized to receive members into this church [Mill Creek] in the settlement of Mashaks Creek and on the waters of Cumberland River as far as Gainsboro, Tenn.[24]

and again,

> Petition Mt. Pleasant, Poplar Springs, Sinking Springs to constitute a church on waters on Mashack Creek at a new meeting house at John B. Pages.[25]

We cannot assume that there was ever an early meeting house at Wards Branch, as the custom was at that time for the *"arms"* to meet in the house of one of their members.

Historical records back up this assumption, for we find John Mulkey conducting such a service in the house of Williams Sims[26] on the

---

[24] *Minutes of the Mill Creek Baptist Church*, No. 2, (June, 1841)

[25] *Ibid*, (March, 3rd Saturday, 1859)

[26] W.C. Rogers, *Recollections of Men of Faith*, p.224

Cumberland River in 1809 (Sims later donating the land for what would become the Cumberland River Baptist Church in 1818).[27]

What Became of the Church at Wards Branch?

Although the author has located no physical documents that prove this claim, it is, however, his opinion that the church at Wards Branch, after their disappearance from the Stockton Valley Association's records of 1807, followed the principles of the *Restoration Movement* and voluntarily withdrew from the Baptist Association at about the same time of John and Philip Mulkey, and formed themselves into a church after the New Testament pattern, and has continued as such through the years in what is now known as the Sulphur Ridge church of Christ. Oral history, and other facts that will be noted later in this chapter, both support this assumption.

The earliest known historical record of the Sulphur Ridge church of Christ is dated September 25, 1927. This document is an early ledger book kept by the church, beginning at that date, and continuing through July of 1952. The old ledger book is at this writing (1996) in the possession of Mr. and Mrs. Harlie Strode of Tompkinsville.

For the most part, the old ledger book contains the financial transactions of the church at Sulphur Ridge through those years (collections and expenses), however, the book does begin by naming the church and its membership (104 names), including the names of those men who were selected as elders and deacons. Following is transcribed the opening remarks of the ledger book.[28]

Sept. 25, 1927
Sulphur Ridge

---

[27] *Pioneer Baptist Church Records of South-Central Kentucky and the Upper Cumberland of Tennessee 1799-1899*, p.452

[28] The following was written in script, in pencil. In some cases the exact letters are difficult to determine. Some of the names may be misspelled, and some are obviously repeated, but all are transcribed as they were originally recorded.

The following is a record of the church of Christ at Sulphur Ridge Monroe Co. Ky. as voted on and adopted by the members of said church.

The officers elected are as follows:

For Elders - Bro E.T. Petett, Bro. S.M. Vance

For Deacons - Bro. Benton Bartley, Bro. C.W. Murray

For Treasurer - Bro. A.K. Graves

Following is the names of those who have placed their membership at this place - Elner Bartley, Lynn Slaughter, Maud Bartley, Ralph Bartley, Cora Cloyd, Ida Meadows, Omer Dodson, Bertha May Slaughter, Carl Bartley, Velma Slaughter, Bina Bartley, Olene Bartley, Lizzie Dodson, Ruby Bartley, Mary Susan Petett, O.H. Graves, Sallie Graves, Olah Graves, Opal Graves, Alice Lou Graves, Other Bartley, Sally Bedford Bartley, Tommie Murray, Alberta Vance, Delma Bryant, Jessie Bartley, Ree Pitcock, Raymond Bartley, E.M. Bartley, Ethel Bartley, Pearl Bartley, C.H. Murray, Lizzie Murray, Otis Bartley, Jessie Bartley, Fowler Short, Ara Bartley, Zelma Bryant, Davie Cloyd, J.P. Perdieu, Locia Bryant, Erlean Bartley, Floyd Murry, Ree Petett, Mrs. Mary Williams, Anna Williams, Mrs. Joss Bartley, Birtha Williams, Wilmer Boyles, Dick Dotson, Lola Dotson, Dewey Curtis, Eugene Curtis, Clyde Rhoten, Stanley Bryant, Emma Bryant, Bina Strode,[29] Birtis McMillen, Olene ' ' ' ' ' ' [McMillen], Pearl'''''[McMillen], Bessie Strode, J. L. Brumit, Raymond Brumit, Mrs. J.S. Brumit, Georgie Pitcock, Jewel Pitcock, Dona Pitcock, S.M. Vance, Alice Bryant, G.S. Bryant, Mrs. Lizzie Dotson, Cloe Dewberry, Vira Bartley, Eva Bryant [*an "x" is placed left of this name*] W.T. Bartley, Neva Curtis, Mrs. Ethel Bartley, Inell Bartley, Jarene Bartley, H.T. Bartley, A.E. McMillian, Keneth Bartley, Jack

---

[29] At this writing (early 1996) Bina Strode is still a faithful and active member of the church at Sulphur Ridge.

Petett, Robert Geralds, Raymond Counts, Clone McMillian, Millard Meodows, Lola Tompkins,

[30]Mr. Benton Emmert, Miss Geneva Emmert, Miss Aletha Emmert, Mrs. Phebia Emmert, Mrs. Mary Murphy, Mrs. Ina Greer, Mr. U.G. Boyles, Uldene Emmert,

[31]Olivie Emmert, Nadine Geralds, Mildred Hammer, Lucy Blythe, Paul Greer, Anna May Blythe, Paul Hammer, Hazel Meadows.

These written records, however, do not constitute the beginning of the church. Oral history establishes that the church had been in existence for many years prior to the 1927 date.

The first known meeting place of the Sulphur Ridge church of Christ, and consequently where it got its current name, was in an old schoolhouse on the ridge overlooking what is known as the U. G. Boyles house at the intersection of Highways 100 and 214 just west of where the current Sulphur Ridge meetinghouse now stands.

All that remains to mark the location of this early schoolhouse are only a few foundation rocks.

It is interesting to note that early Kentucky land grants indicate that Philip Mulkey owned land along Sulphur Creek that either included, or was adjacent to the land where the old Sulphur Ridge Schoolhouse once stood.[32]

Billy Bartley, 56, a current member (1996) of the Sulphur Ridge church of Christ along with his wife, a daughter, and two sisters, recalls working for U. G. Boyles (an elder member of Sulphur Ridge at the time of the 1927

---

[30] The following names were written at a later time as determined by different handwriting style and different pen.

[31] The following names are in the same handwriting style as those just before them, but in different pen.

[32] *History of the Fitzgeralds and Geralds*, p. (-a-), also accompanying map.

minutes, and on whose land the old schoolhouse once occupied) when he just a young boy, and the elder Boyles remarking: *"This is the place where the old church used to meet years ago,"* indicating that part of the ridge where the foundation stones mark where the school once stood.

Another early member of the Sulphur Ridge church, Raymond Bartley, born in 1912 at Wards Branch, says he can't remember as a child the old schoolhouse on the ridge behind the Boyles house where the church once met, but can remember the older people talking about it.

When the school moved from the ridge, sometime in the 1800's, it occupied a new building that once stood directly across Highway 100 from where the current Sulphur Ridge meetinghouse now stands. By around 1927, when Highway 100 was rerouted (according to Alvin Strode, father of current church treasurer Harlie Strode), a new schoolhouse was built and the old one was donated to the Sulphur Ridge church and moved to the location where the current church building now stands.

The new schoolhouse is still standing at this date (1996), but was converted into a family dwelling after *"country schools"* were done away with in Monroe County.

The old schoolhouse that was donated to the church and moved across the road about 1927, was the first actual meetinghouse that the church had ever owned as far as history is able to determine.

In the early 1950's, that facility was torn down and the current Sulphur Ridge meetinghouse was built.

But there is additional material that lends support to the claim that the Wards Branch Church followed the *Restoration Movement* of the early 1800's.

It is very interesting to note that one of the early members of the Wards Branch Church was Thomas Ray, brother to Elder William Ray who preached for the Kettle Creek Church in Cumberland County.

It can therefore be assumed, that the Wards Branch Church was very early exposed to *Restoration* principles as the Kettle Creek Church was one of the first congregations in the area to withdraw from the Baptists, as indicated from the following records:

> Kettle Creek Church seemed to prosper for a while. In 1802, they reported 33 new members baptized into the church. Matters went well until 1803, at which time the church petitioned the association for "an open communion," which was rejected, because of its "direct opposition" to the rules and constitution of the Green River Association.
> At the 1804 session of the Green River Association it was reported that a majority of Kettle Creek "were fallen into open communion and are excluded."[33]

That same Baptist historical source came to the following conclusion concerning the Kettle Creek Church:

> The Cumberland River Church [near Black's Ferry in Monroe County, Kentucky] was gathered shortly after the Kettle Creek Church was broken up by the "New Light" movement.[34]

Conclusion

While it can never be known for certain at this late date, whether the Sulphur Ridge church of Christ is the continuation of a group of pioneer Christians at Wards Branch which followed the Mulkeys and the churches of Mill Creek and Brimstone in an attempt to restore the church of the New Testament pattern, such an assumption is certainly not far-fetched, and not without at least some historical support.

---

[33] *Pioneer Baptist Church Records of South-Central Kentucky and the Upper Cumberland of Tennessee 1799-1899*, p. 465.
[34] *Ibid*, p. 452.

Perhaps the strongest argument in favor of this assumption is the fact that, looking at it from the context of a church-arrangement, the only group that is known to have continued as a Baptist Church, from either the Mill Creek congregation, or its *"arms"* was the minority that went off to establish the second Mill Creek Baptist Church after the division of 1809.

The author, however, does not accept the explanation of some Baptist historians that the church at Wards Branch simply dissolved. This was a period of great religious revival. Baptist records well indicate this, as they show that membership numbers in Kentucky between the years of 1800 and 1810 increased from 5,119 to 16,650.[35]

Clearly, this was a period of religious growth, not decline. In those instances where Baptists did lose numbers, they were losing them to the *Restoration Movement*, not apathy.

Obviously, much is left to speculation concerning the Brimstone and Wards Branch churches. But this is not the case with the Mill Creek Baptist Church itself.

In our next chapter we will reveal the events that led to the division of that body of pioneer Baptists.

---

[35] Leo Taylor Crismon, *Baptists in Kentucky, 1776-1976, A Bicentennial Volume*, p. 147.

*"Awake, awake, put on strength,
O arm of the Lord;
Awake as in the ancient days,
in the generations of old."*

Isaiah 51:9

A History of the Mill Creek ("Old Mulkey") Church
Tompkinsville, Kentucky

Chapter 5

John Mulkey's Hard Decisions

There were a lot ways in which the preachers in John Mulkey's day were very much different from preachers today. Seldom did these men earn a living preaching the Gospel, and seldom were they confined to just one local congregation.

As noted in the previous chapter, it was the philosophy of the Baptists at the turn of the 1800's to plant a church in one particular region, then immediately begin to extend the bounds of that church by constituting what they called *"arms"* or *"branches"* throughout the community.

As the mother church extended her bounds, often, it was up to the minister of that mother church to visit all these extensions and handle the preaching; visiting one church this week of the month, another the next week, and so on. In fact, the local minister of the original church might be called upon to preach at several different *"arms"* or *"branches,"* all in the same week.

However, not only did the minister serve the extensions of his own church, he might also be called upon to preach for churches outside of his own immediate area, especially if there was a lack of capable preachers in the area.

Such appears to have been the life that John Mulkey led in his ministry of the early 1800's.

In the records of the early Mill Creek Church we find that Mulkey's services were requested by two churches outside the Mill Creek area to come and preach for them twice a month.

> September, 2nd Saturday, 1800 - ...Requests from Churches on Pitman's Creek and in Russels Settlement complyed [sic] with this Church gives up her pasture [sic] the first and third Sunday in every month to attend them churches...[1]

The Pitman's Creek Church was located in what is known today as Taylor County, Kentucky, a considerable distance for Mulkey to have to travel.

Modern Baptists historians consider that this was common practice among the pioneer Baptist churches, however.

> A custom which prevailed among the pioneer Baptists, and one that is frequently mentioned in the association records of the Eastern U.S., was to establish branches or "arms" of the parent church in the surrounding country to make available their preacher to the scattered groups of Baptists.
>
> Due to the difficult conditions that existed in that day, it was easier for the minister to visit these "arms" than for the members to assemble at one central location.
>
> Pitman's Creek Church wrote to Mill Creek Church in Monroe County for the use of their minister, John Mulkey, on the first and third Sundays in each month. This involved considerable travel on the part of the minister but it was the acceptable "way" at that time.
>
> When the "branch" or "arm" became strong enough, they were permitted to conduct business meetings, which was [sic] sanctioned by the mother church...[2]

---

[1] *Minutes of the Mill Creek Baptist Church*, (September 1800), p. 20.

[2] Cawthorn, Warnell, *Pioneer Baptist Church Records of South-Central Kentucky and the Upper Cumberland of Tennessee 1799-1899* , p. 206. 76

Such requests often indicated the lack of adequate preachers available at that time, but they also often inferred the high esteem the church had for the preacher they requested.

Not only did Mulkey answer the request at Pitman's Creek for his services, it also appears from early church records that he continued that relationship for some time, as the following minutes reveal.

> "The Church directs the clerk to draw up a subscription for Brother Mulkey to serve the church as a minister...," whereupon the clerk recorded: "a subscription was drawn up for the purpose of satisfying Brother John Mulkey for attending the church monthly one year." The total collected was $66.00. John Mulkey's name Appears as moderator on June 4, 1808. In December 1808, a committee was appointed to "hire a Negro boy of brother Richardson for brother Mulkey and report next meeting."[3]

In addition to preaching duties, John Mulkey also helped gather other churches outside the realm of the Mill Creek Baptist Church in Monroe County.

One of those churches he helped establish was the Concord Baptist Church in Barren County, Kentucky.

> Concord was first known as Trace Creek Church. It appears to have been gathered, although not constituted, about 1800 by John Mulkey who was its first pastor.[4]
>
> ...John Mulkey and Cornelius Deweese pastored the [Concord] church before the recognized organization date of 1811.
> ...Among the ministers of the [Concord] church were: John Mulkey, Cornelius Deweese, Augustine Clayton, John Baker, Isaac Tracey, Seth Bradshaw and R. H. Payne.[5]

---

[3] *Pioneer Baptist Church Records of South-Central Kentucky and the Upper Cumberland of Tennessee 1799-1899*, p. 434.

[4] *Ibid*, p. 83.

[5] Cecil E. Goode, *Barren County Heritage*, "Churches", p. 170.

Realizing the great need for his services, the Mill Creek Church opened the door for John Mulkey to do such "outside" preaching in a business meeting in April 1803.

> ...Brother John Mulkey Set at liberty to go whersover [sic] he may think proper.[6]

John Mulkey Rejects Unconditional Election

It was during one such *"outside"* preaching service that John Mulkey was first convinced that at least a portion of the Baptist doctrine that he had dedicated his life to promote was in direct opposition to the scriptures.

The incident took place while Mulkey was preaching at the William Sims house on the Cumberland River in 1809.

The gathering at the Sims house was a possible *"arm"* of the Mill Creek Church. It is even possible that the following two minutes from the Mill Creek Church could pertain to the church that was meeting at the William Sims house, instead of the Brimstone Church, as we noted in our previous chapter [pages 58-59], although this is uncertain:

> Saturday, June 12,1802 - A letter from a part of this Church on Mill Creek South of Cumberland River for helps in order to Inquire into their fitness for constitution. Agree to answer them next meeting...[7]

> Saturday, July 10, 1802 - The Church give up part of the Church South of Cumberland River for constitution if found fit when a presbytery for that purpose is Asurtained [sic]...[8]

This much is known, however, that the church was later known as the Cumberland River Baptist Church which was located on land donated by William Sims in 1818.

---

[6] *Minutes of the Mill Creek Baptist Church*, (April, 1803), p. 40.
[7] *Ibid*, (June 12, 1802), pp. 34-35.
[8] *Ibid*, (July 10, 1802), p. 35.

The Cumberland River Baptist Church of Monroe County was located on the land of Williams Sims. An entry in the Cumberland County Deed Book C, pg. 338 states:

"This Indenture made and entered this sixth Day of Sept. One thousand eight and seventeen between Williams Sims of the County of Cumberland and state of Kentucky of the one part and Jesse Martin and John Page trustees of the Cumberland Baptist Church and the County and state of the other part witnesseth that the said William Sims hath this day for the inconsideration of the sum of six dollars to him in hand paid, the receipt is hereby fully acknowledged hath bargained sold unto the said trustees above mentioned to a certain tract of ground containing one hundred acres to include the Cumberland Baptist Meeting House and bounded as follows..."

"Delivered to John Page the 8th Day of June 1818" [9]

Other documents indicate that the Cumberland River Baptist Church was established in the 1800's at Black' Ferry, previously known as Jackson's Ferry and Biggerstaff Ferry, in Cumberland County, Kentucky.[10]

Those same records indicate that Williams Sims owned land in the Turkey Neck Bend area of the Cumberland River; that land today being on both sides of the Monroe County-Cumberland County line.

The Cumberland River Baptist Church was listed as a member of the Stockton Valley Association in 1806, sending as messengers Levi Rhoden, A. Sims, and A. Wood, listing a membership of 25. William Sims appears as a messenger to the Association's meeting in 1816, where the church indicated a membership of 49.

The account of the incident at the Sims house involving John Mulkey was recorded by the pen of Elder Isaac T. Reneau [noted preacher in the *Restoration Movement*] and appeared in a book Written by W.C. Rogers in 1889. Rogers' book covered the careers of several of the Restoration

---

[9] *Pioneer Baptist Church Records of South-Central Kentucky and the Upper Cumberland of Tennessee 1799-1899*, p. 452.

[10] *History of the Fitzgeralds and Geralds*, p. (-a-), also accompanying map.

preachers and included the account of John Mulkey at the Sims house in his chapter on John Newton Mulkey, son of John Mulkey.

There has been a direct line of preachers in the Mulkey family for about one hundred and fifty years. Philip Mulkey, the great•grandfather of John N. Mulkey, was a Baptist preacher in the Meherian Association in 1756, one hundred and twenty-six years ago (Temple's Hist. Vir. Baptists, page 222.)

But, according to others, he had been a "respectable and successful preacher for many years." If it required twenty-four years of mental and physical labor to evaluate him "reputable" eminence, we have the one hundred and fifty. For his son, grandson and great-grandson continued the line till the death of the great-grandson [John Newton Mulkey] in 1882.

Philip Mulkey's son Jonathan was born, probably in South Carolina, and perhaps commenced preaching in that State. But about the year 1780 he, Wm. Reneau and other ministers and brethren, some from Carolina, and some from Virginia, emigrated [sic] to East Tennessee and organized a Baptist Church on Boone's Creek. The church is now called "Buffalo Ridge" (Benedict's Hist. Baptists, page 791).

Jonathan Mulkey was one of the most pious and influential preachers in Tennessee, and made a better mold of character in the Baptist churches than any other man in the State. And he lived to enjoy in his old age the privilege of being associated with his father and his son John in preaching in the same pulpit and on the same day.

Jonathan Mulkey's son John was born in South Carolina, Jan. 14, 1773, and commenced preaching in East Tennessee in the twentieth year of his age, and in a few years became one of the finest pulpit orators in the State. But near the beginning of the present century [1800] he and his brother Philip emigrated [sic] to Kentucky, and settled on Mill Creek, two miles southeast of Tompkinsville, and they soon obtained "a good degree and great boldness in the faith."

But in the year 1809, the following incident occurred: While John Mulkey was preaching on the 10th chapter of John, in William Sims' house, on the Cumberland River, and making one of his strongest efforts to establish Calvinism, his own argument convinced himself that the doctrine was false. This roused up the powers of his great mind, and caused him to "express a change in his sentiments on unconditional election and some other subjects." This caused great confusion in the Mill Creek Church, and also through the Stockton's Valley Association. They immediately charged him with "heresy," and cited him to appear at the August meeting for 1809, to answer the charge. But not finding him guilty at the August meeting, they agreed to call on five other churches for "help" in the next trial at the October meeting, as requested, and after investigating the charge, the proposition was made for "all that justify Bro. Mulkey to raise their right hands." But as the majority were [sic] in his favor, no more could be done then than continue the suit till the second Saturday in November. In the November trial, John Mulkey proposed to "drop all disputes and bear with one another," but they replied, "Never, till you come back to the very ground from which you started." He then proposed a dissolution of the church, to which all agreed; and as many as wished to continue on their old platform, enrolled their names as 'The Church." But John Mulkey, and all that went with him in the division, met together on the third Saturday in November, 1809, and after prayer organized a church on *"the Bible alone"* - the Bible without human creed, confession of faith, or book of discipline.

After the start of the Restoration, John and Philip Mulkey sowed the good seed broadcast over all the land, and though the beginning was small, they soon prepared a great host for the consummate restoration of the first form, order, work, and life of the church which was built on the *"Rock."* And though it was small at the beginning, it is now very large - "it has begirt the earth around."...[11]

But this wasn't the first time that John Mulkey had been faced with concerns over the *Calvinistic* doctrine of *Unconditional Election.* The subject had already been discussed at a business meeting of the Mill Creek Baptist Church as early as October 1803.

---

[11] W.C. Rogers, *Recollections of Men of Faith*, P. 223-225.

Beginning with the October 1803 meeting, the congregation considered the *"Election"* language of their church covenant, and finally resolved to drop that part and adopt the language of the Green River Association in February 1804 [see "Articles of Faith of the Green River Association" on page 31 of this book].

Modern Baptist historians offer these comments:

> John Mulkey attempted to strike a moderate position; he did not wholly concur with the extreme Calvinists who simply waited for the invasion of God's spirit, or with some of the others who used the Scriptures mechanically in conversion. In joining the Green River Association, he was among those who preached the "primitive gospel" pattern of love and the doctrine of the new birth.
>
> The church covenant of Mill Creek, which John and Philip Mulkey brought from the Big Pigeon Baptist Church in East Tennessee in 1797, was Calvinistic in principle stating [see copy of *"The Old Covenant of Mill Creek Baptist Church"* on page 35 of this book] "...particular election of Grace by predestination of God in Christ Jesus."
>
> Big Pigeon Baptist Church was a member of the Holston Association which had adopted the principles of the Philadelphia Association.
>
> Under Mulkey's leadership the Mill Creek Church pulled away from the rigid Calvinistic principle in their church covenant. In October 1803, Mill Creek recorded the following entry in their minutes - "Some things in our church covenant thought necessary to erase and to adopt the language of the articles of the Green River Association."[12]

Actually, the decision of the Mill Creek church concerning the adoption of the language of the Green River Association at the October 1803 meeting was that they, *"agreed to consider of it to next meeting."* [13]

---

[12] *Pioneer Baptist Church Records of South-Central Kentucky and the Upper Cumberland of Tennessee 1799-1899*, p. 435.

[13] *Minutes of the Mill Creek Baptist Church*, (October, 1803), p. 45.

The subject was again brought up at the November 1803 meeting, but *"laid over,"* and again in the December 1803 meeting where is was *"Still laid over,"* and in January 1804 where *"John Mulkey, Benjamin Gist Sr., John Wood, Obadiah Howard, Francess Baxter a committe to arrange matter and present it next meeting in course."*

Finally, in February 1804, the Mill Creek Church agreed to adopt the language of the Green River Association *"with some particulars added thereunto."* [those particulars that were added not recorded].

Regardless of what adjustments that were made to the old covenant of the Mill Creek Church in 1803 and 1804 concerning the Calvinistic teaching of *"Election",* they were obviously not satisfactory as far as John Mulkey was concerned when he preached at the Sims place in 1809.

Baptist historians claim that the churches of the Green River Association were not Calvinist in their teaching.

> ...Another point that was dropped by the Green River Baptists was that of "particular election of Grace." This was a Calvinistic view on doctrine coming from the Philadelphia Association of 1742. All of the first Baptist associations in Kentucky and Tennessee refer to the Philadelphia Confession of faith in their constitution except the Separate Baptists which were leery of confessions of faith, fearing that these might come to tyrannize over the conscience. But in time they did accept to form the United Baptists group and after it had been made clear that liberty would be allowed, as to the interpretation of certain items in the confession.[14]

The same is also implied concerning the churches that formed the Stockton Valley Association.

In commenting upon the 4th Article of Faith of the Rennix Creek (Salem) Church in Cumberland County, Kentucky, which reads:

---

[14] *Pioneer Baptist Church Records of South-Central Kentucky and the Upper Cumberland of Tennessee 1799-1899*, p. 424.

> ...4th We believe the doctrine of Election and the Final Preservation of the Saints through Grace and that the happyness [sic] of the Righteous and the Punishment of the wicked will be Eternal.[15]

Modern Baptist historians make the following comment:

> The confessions of faith or doctrinal statements adopted by the early associations were generally, but not always followed by the affiliating churches.
> The reader will notice the 4th Article of Faith [see above quote], that the doctrine of "election" is mentioned. The articles of Faith of both the Green River and Stockton Valley Associations made no provision for unconditional election.
> Rennix Creek and Mill Creek Churches are the only early churches in the Stockton Valley Association that have presently been found that made mention of this Calvinistic principle. Mill Creek dropped their "particular election" and adopted the language of the Articles of Faith of the Green River Association in October 1803. [16]

Apparently, however, they did not go far enough, else why would John Mulkey have come to the conclusion that he did in 1809 at the William Sims house?

From his own writings years later, we know for a fact that *"unconditional election"* was the primary issue that John Mulkey and the minority of the Mill Creek Church differed on in the November 1809 division.

> ...it is generally well known, that some years ago a dissatisfaction took the doctrine of unconditional Election, and some other subjects; which led to much disputation, and finally terminated in an entire

---

[15] *Pioneer Baptist Church Records of South-Central Kentucky and the Upper Cumberland of Tennessee 1799-1899*, p. 477.
[16] *Ibid*, p. 478.

separation of myself and a number of others from the Baptist Church.[17]

We must, therefore, assume that even if the physical documents of these early Baptist Churches didn't follow the *Calvinistic* doctrine of *"Election"*, something in their teaching did. Otherwise, wherein did John Mulkey and the Mill Creek Church differ on the subject?

Following the awakening that John Mulkey underwent at the Sims place, he is said to have returned to the Mill Creek Church, having resolved the following:

> ... Our only creed should be Christ. Our only book the Bible. Our only rule of conduct: that life laid down by the Master himself. Too many times have we let party spirit and human pride mar the opportunity to join hands with all Christians and declare the common faith in the risen Lord. We Baptists could take the lead in restoring a New Testament faith and a New Testament freedom to our country that now stands on the brink of being plunged again into a second war for independence, an independence that many of our people fought and died to claim. But we are in danger of losing something far more important than our national independence. Where there is slavery of men's minds I say that the bonds must be broken. Where there are restrictions on a man's faith I say the fetters must be flayed asunder. Let us forget our petty doctrines and our pompous confessions and kneel before the Lord himself in sackcloth and ashes, repenting of our sins and pledging restitution for our limiting the ministry of Him who came that we might have life and have it more abundantly. Let us lay aside our belief that some are saved and some are damned even before the world began. If that were so, then why are we here in this wilderness of Kentucky trying to bring up our offspring in the ways of the Lord. If He knows who is to be saved and who is to be lost, all

---

[17] John Mulkey, *"A Circular Letter Addressed to the Christian Churches in the Western Country"* [Printed by] J.A. Woodson, Glasgow, Ky. 1821, (Copy in Christian Theological Seminary Library, Indianapolis, IN).

human efforts are of no avail and our work is but abomination and a farce![18]

This was the very teaching that got John Mulkey in hot water with Elder John Wood and the minority of the Mill Creek Church and the Stockton Valley Association. This new doctrine of Mulkey's was what resulted in his trials and the subsequent breakup of the Mill Creek Baptist Church.

But the *Calvinistic* doctrine of *"Election"* wasn't the only point in which Mulkey differed with the Baptists.

Association Questions

As early as June 8, 1805, we find that questions were being asked at the Mill Creek Church concerning the scriptural authority of Associations.

> ...Appointed Brethren John Mulkey, Francess Baxter, and John Graston to attend [Green River] association at Mt. Tabor on the 4th Saturday in July next.
>
> The church agrees to send a remonstrance against the 14th article of the last year's minutes, viz the query from Beaver Creek.
>
> Also a query to this effect - What authority have we in the Word of God for a [sic] association?[19]

Mention is again made concerning *"the scriptural authority of an association"* in the August 1806 minutes,[20] although nothing is mentioned throughout the remainder of the minute book concerning any decision that the church made.

Perhaps the fact that that part of the Mill Creek Church which split off from the Baptists, as well as the *"arms"* at both Brimstone and Ward Branch (Meshack Creek) were not mentioned in the minutes of any of the Baptist Associations following the division of 1809 (Wards Branch not appearing after 1807; Brimstone not represented after 1808, being formally excluded

---

[18] E. Clayton Gooden, *A Fork in the Road*, p. 159.
[19] *Minutes of the Mill Creek Baptist Church*, (June 8, 1805), p. 57.
[20] *Ibid*, (August 1806), p. 63.

by the Stockton Valley Association in 1812) is evidence enough to show that these churches who were involved in the *Restoration Movement* considered them unscriptural.

We know that this was the case with Baptist churches in the future.

Years later, Alexander Campbell (a leading figure in the *Restoration Movement*, first from among the Presbyterians, and later from the Baptists) included much on the subject of Associations in his periodical, *The Christian Baptist* (1823-1830). In those writings, Campbell, through the reprinting of articles dealing with Associations, reveals the thinking of those churches involved in the *Restoration Movement* concerning the subject of these man-made organizations.

While it is not within the scope of this work to reprint every article in that publication that dealt with the subject of Baptist Associations, it will serve the reader in gaining a better understanding of the issue to observe two; the first a letter addressed to the Concord Baptist Association of Tennessee, the second, a letter of resolution from the Boon Creek Association of Baptists in Kentucky.

May 7, 1827.
Deferred Articles

The following letter is from one of the most intelligent churches in the western states with which we are acquainted. It was addressed to a very respectable Baptist Association in the state of Tennessee, and we are happy to learn that this Association had so much intelligence and liberality as to accept it as the platform and basis of a union with it and the church who wrote it. So long as associations are kept up, we think that were they to act up to the principles herein stated and recognized, much less injury could result to the christian community from their meetings than has hitherto been the result of them. This is a good step and a rapid advance towards the introduction of a better order of things. - Ed. [Alexander Campbell]

The Church of Jesus Christ at Nashville, to the Concord Association, sendeth Christian Salutation.

Dear Brethren, - After an interval of two years, we again address you by letter and messengers. Various circumstances induced us last year not to unite ourselves to any association, which circumstances it is not necessary to enumerate. We again present ourselves before you, and request to be admitted into your body.

Deeming it perfectly necessary that we distinctly understand each other, upon forming this union, we think it proper to state our sentiments concerning associations, and the relation they bear to the churches composing them.

Your code of government, as published in 1825, declares that the association "shall have no power to Lord it over God's heritage, neither shall it have any ecclesiastical power, or infringe upon the internal rights of the churches." To all this we cheerfully consent, and consider it an expression of our own feelings. We may not, however, understand it alike, and will therefore beg leave to exhibit our views of it.

We understand this sentence as saying, that the association has no power to determine what any church shall receive as her creed; or whether she shall have any creed or confession at all, other than the bible; and consequently that she has no power so to lord it over God's heritage, as to condemn any church for holding or teaching any scriptural truths, though at variance with the opinions of this body concerning such truths.

In this view of the subject, we presume it will not be required of us to subscribe to any human instrument of union, as the test of our doctrine or practice. For we cannot but believe, that the Holy Bible is as plain in expressing its own truth as it ought to have been; and consequently that no man can express more clearly than it does, what we are to believe and practise [sic]. If this be true, (and we presume it will not be denied,) it is useless for us, as a church, or for any other body, to hold up a twinkling taper to give light to the world, when the sun shines in his meridian splendor. If the fear of

God and the love of the brethren will not hold the disciples in union, upon the one foundation, we may forever despair of any such instruments of union as creeds and confessions of faith obtaining so desirable an end.

Again - We understand the "constitution" of your body as saying, when it declares the association "shall have no ecclesiastical power," &c. that the association does not intend to interfere with any of the *internal rights* of the churches. That is to say: the association has no power to interfere with the *order, doctrine, government,* or *practice,* of any church, *governed in all,* by the great charter of our religious privileges - the *New* Testament of our blessed Lord and Saviour [sic] Jesus Christ. We consider all these to be the "internal rights of the churches" - rights given them by the Great Head of the church - rights expressly defined and limited by Him, "in whom are hid all the treasures of wisdom and knowledge;" and, therefore, rights which are inalienable, and over which no body of men on earth has any control. In short, we consider ourselves at liberty to appoint our own teacher or teachers, and all other officers, without molestation or assistance from any; and to judge for ourselves, when the sentiments delivered by our teachers, so appointed, are contained in the Holy Bible; without acknowledging the right of any others to interfere in the judicial investigation of such sentiments.

Indeed, brethren, we look upon your "constitution" as guaranteeing to every church connected with it, a full, free, and unmolested liberty of conscience - a liberty unshackled by any authority, except his who has set his people free; a liberty that is not, and will not be, used as a cloak for licentiousness by any one [sic] who fears God, and desires to walk by the light of the truth; and a liberty which none other than God who gave it has any right to destroy, and which this association, most certainly, will never assail.

It is our desire, beloved brethren, to live harmoniously with all our brethren; and while we acknowledge ourselves to be "of you," we think that these are the only principles on which unity can be maintained.

We do not consider ourselves the guardians of the public faith; nor as having any right to direct what any shall believe. Error requires not human efforts to overthrow it: the exhibition of the truth in its simplicity, has ever been found, in the hands of God, a weapon most mighty to the pulling down of strong holds.

We trust, brethren, that while we deny the authority of men in matters of religion, we feel bound to endeavor to ascertain the will of our glorious chief; and so far as we know it, to observe it. We are far from supposing that all is known, at the present day, of the Records of Heaven, that we can be known; and are therefore willing to learn "what is truth," whoever be the instrument of pointing us to it. That there yet remains much to be known concerning divine things we must believe; for "if any man thinks he knows any thing [sic], he knows nothing yet as he ought to know."[21]

* * *

Extract from the Minutes of the Boon Creek Association of Baptists in Kentucky, for the present year.

"On motion, The following remarks and resolution were adopted in answer to the request from several churches composing this association, for an amendment of her constitution, so as to make it more scriptural, or compatible with the word of God, viz. This association having taken into consideration the request of some of the churches for an amendment of her constitution, after mature deliberation, she is decidedly of opinion that the word of God does not authorise [sic] or prescribe any form of constitution for an association in our present organized state. (Our constitution we have caused to be printed in those minutes, for the inspection of the churches making up their opinions to the next association;) but we do believe that the word of God authorises [sic] the assembling of saints together for his worship; we therefore recommend to the churches an abolition of the present constitution, and in lieu thereof, adoption of this resolution:

Resolved, That we, the churches of Jesus Christ, believing the scriptures of the Old and New Testaments to be the word of God, and

---

[21] Alexander Campbell, *The Christian Baptist*, (May 7, 1827), Vol. 4, No. 10, p. 330.

the only rule of faith and obedience given by the Great Head of the Church for its government, do agree to meet annually on every 3d Saturday, Lord's day, and Monday in September of each year, for the worship of God; and on such occasions voluntarily communicate the state of religion amongst us by letter and messengers."

This is a most excellent substitute for the annual advisory councils and legislative deliberations of a church representative of churches. Any number of christians [sic] who please to meet at any time or place for such purposes as the Boon Creek association contemplates, has all the authority which reason and Revelation make necessary to acceptable service. Instead of a judicial court of Inquiry, and of resolves, we have a meeting of fellow Christians for prayer and praise and thanksgiving, for mutual exhortation and edification. It would be a happy era in the history of Christianity if all ecclesiastical courts, whether papistical [sic], Episcopalian [sic], Presbyterian [sic], independent, or any thing [sic] else would regenerate themselves into worshipping [sic] assemblies.[22]

* * *

It is interesting to note that the same sentiments that are revealed in the above extracts from Alexander Campbell's *The Christian Baptist* concerning Baptist Associations were being contended for years earlier by John Mulkey.

Speaking of the views that he held, and those who followed him in the division of the Mill Creek Church in 1809, Mulkey wrote to the churches in general in 1821:

> ...we finally concluded that all human creeds and confessions of faith were the works of fallible man and consequently they were imperfect and contradictory to each other and also that they had been the cause of many, if not most of the divisions in the church of God; likewise that they all had their zealous advocates, and, of course were

---

[22] Alexander Campbell, *The Christian Baptist*, (December 1, 1828), Vol. 6, No. 5, p. 508.

calculated to divide Christians, and keep them apart. And further, believing that Christ is the great head of the church and King of Zion, the only Christian lawgiver, and that he had given a sufficiency of laws, rules and regulations, for the government of his church and people. We proceeded to unite ourselves as a Christian Society, agreeable to our best views of the Gospel; having, as we hoped first given to our Lord - we then gave ourselves to each other, by the will of God, to be subject to Christ and to each other in the Gospel, taking the Holy Scriptures as the only rule of our faith and practice, we therefore receive all whom we believe Christ has received, with the exception only of such as have been excluded from other societies, for immoral conduct; in that case we esteem it our duty, first to confess their faith to their brethren whom they offended: but if any are cast off using this religious liberty, we freely receive them, - believing that Christ has made them free, and that liberty of conscience is a right that God has conferred on his intelligent creatures and none has the right to take it from them, seeing that they are to account to God alone, for their religious conduct...[23]

---

[23] John Mulkey, "*A Circular Letter Addressed to the Christian Churches in the Western Country*" [printed by] J.A. Woodson, Glasgow, Ky. 1821, (Copy in Christian Theological Seminary Library, Indianapolis, I N) .

A History of the Mill Creek ("Old Mulkey") Church
Tompkinsville, Kentucky

Chapter 6

After the Division of 1809

We have now come full circle from where we started in Chapter 1 of this book; back to the division of the Mill Creek Baptist Church on November 18, 1809.

In our previous chapters we have revealed that John and Philip Mulkey were not only dedicated men, they were also dedicated Baptists.

It seemed a small matter for them to gather their families and leave the relative safety of East Tennessee in the late 1700's and journey into the wilderness of Kentucky and into unknown dangers.

But these faithful men were true *"evangelists"* and felt it their God-given duty to exercise their abilities in those areas that were before deprived of capable preaching.

And not enough is said of their wives and children, and how that they unselfishly followed their husbands and fathers in their pursuits, supporting them in both spirit and deed.

More often than not, pioneer preachers were gone from home fulfilling their duties to desolate churches, while the everyday chores of carving out a living in the wilderness of Kentucky was left to their family that remained at home. As we have before stated, these preachers didn't earn a living preaching; that was left for them and their families to accomplish in addition to their efforts of promoting the Christian religion.

Crops had to be planted, tended, and then harvested. Livestock had to be cared for. Firewood had to be felled, cut, split, and stockpiled within easy access. All of these duties often fell upon the families of these dedicated preachers.

It was indeed a hard life. But apparently, they never considered it should be any other way.

It was this kind of attitude, service, and dedication that earned the Mulkey families the respect of the people that were associated with them.

Consequently, the Mulkeys became prominent leaders in the Baptist organization in Southern Kentucky and Northern Tennessee. They gathered churches where none existed before, established Baptist Associations to accommodate and solidify those churches where none were needed before, and they gave every fiber of their very being to see to it that the religion of Jesus Christ did not suffer in the region in which they lived.

In consideration of these matters, understanding as best we can how close-knit that the pioneer families must have been drawn together, only serves to give us some idea of how difficult it must have been when their interpretation of the scriptures led them in different directions.

Friends were divided, families were split; each as harshly as so many double-bladed axes had severed so many pieces of oak and hickory firewood on too many cold winter mornings in the Mill Creek and surrounding settlements.

Why?

John Mulkey gives us his defense:

> ...If we are duly engaged in doing his will, and following the Savior, we shall know the shepherd's voice, and shall not follow strangers; we shall delight in things that become sound doctrine, and love all men and pity and pray for worst enemies. Finally our light will shine and trust will prevail. Indeed, brethren, we have reason to rejoice that notwithstanding the floods of opposition and torrents of abuse that have poured forth from various quarters, yet truth is prevailing. Gospel light is shining. Error and sectarian bigotry is in many instances giving way; and the Kingdom of the Redeemer is spreading.
>
> For these things we should be truly thankful, and willingly suffer for his name's sake; yea, and rejoice in our persecutions, which we bear

for truth's sake. Our Lord foretold us these things, and directs us to rejoice and be exceeding glad for so persecuted they the prophets which were before you dear brethren; you know that these things have been the lot of the faithful in all ages. We ought to be patient under all these things, when our enemies charge us with denying the Savior, why need we mind that, seeing we know whom we have believed; yea we know him and the power of his resurrection, and the fellowship of his sufferings. When they charge us with denying his blood, we know its efficacy on our hearts that it purifies and cleanses from all sin. And while our adversaries charge us with making Christ a part of our Savior, and denying the efficacy of his blood, some of them deny that Christ died in any special sense, for any but a part of the human race; and also deny that his blood cleanses from all sin while we are well assured that he has died in the most proper and unlimited sense, for the sins of the whole world, and we exult in the efficacy of that blood, which does cleanse the believer from all sin. But it makes but little difference what we are charged with, our trust is in God, and those who trust in man or maketh flesh their arm are accursed.

Dear Brethren, let us bear all things with patience and resignation, knowing that men are not to be our judges; let us be sincerely thankful for the late revival of God's work among us, and steadily cherish the same and be steadfast, unmovable, always abounding in the work of the Lord, all the powers of darkness will be engaged to check this glorious work; and one thing will certainly be aimed at, and that will be to draw your attention to other subjects, and if possible to keep you from suitable engagements for the salvation of precious souls. The instruments that God makes use of in carrying on his work will be as marks for the enemy to shoot at from every quarter. But if we keep our eye fixed on the Savior they can do us no harm, but will often unintentionally do us good. For my own part I can truly say these things have sometimes been a great comfort to me; and when reproaches and slanders have been flying, thick on every side, my soul has been happily feasting on the love of God and a spirit to pity and pray for my persecutors, and sometimes my friends have thought that I should certainly be overwhelmed. I could still say with Paul that none of these things move me, neither count I my life as dear to myself. So that I may finish my course with you and the ministry, and that I may have received the Lord Jesus to testify the Gospel of the Grace of God. Again I say with the same servant of God, after the way they call heresy so worship I the God of my fathers believing all things that are written in the law and the prophets.

And now, brethren, I commend you to God, and the word of his grace, which is able to build you up, and give you an inheritance among all them that are sanctified. The grace of our Lord Jesus Christ be with you all. Amen.

I am your servant,
For Jesus' sake,
John Mulkey [1]

If there were one thing that the Mulkeys held more precious than anything else - be it friends, family, or even life itself - it was TRUTH.

They would stand for it, they would fight for it, and they would willingly have died for it. It was to them the *"pearl of great price."*

How else can we explain the stand that they took for what they believed? In the eyes of today's society, it was not a profitable move for John and Philip Mulkey in their current circumstances. True, they did carry the majority vote at the Mill Creek Church and retain possession of the building, but look at what they lost.

The Mulkeys had been pillars in the Baptist community in Southern Kentucky and Northern Tennessee. Not only were they highly regarded by the individual churches they served, they were also held in similar high esteem in the Baptist Associations they had helped to establish. But they gave all that up, and for what? For what they considered was TRUTH, and nothing else.

In years to come the *Restoration Movement* would grow in strength and popularity. But this certainly wasn't the case in 1809. John and Philip

---

[1] John Mulkey, *"A Circular Letter Addressed to the Christian Churches in the Western Country"* [printed by] J.A. Woodson, Glasgow, Ky. 1821, (Copy in Christian Theological Seminary Library, Indianapolis, IN).

Mulkey were on the cutting edge of the *Restoration*, two of the first to make a stand for *"the Ancient Order of Things."*

It is a difficult task to trace the history of John and Philip Mulkey after the division of the Mill Creek Church in 1809. Documentation concerning their efforts in the *Restoration* are few, and far between.

However, due to preserved documents throughout Kentucky and Tennessee during the early years of this move to restore New Testament Christianity, we do get glimpses of the activity of both John and Philip Mulkey, as well as their brother Isaac Mulkey.

One of the most widely circulated religious papers in Kentucky during the middle 1800's was Barton W. Stone's *Christian Messenger*, a periodical that was published by Stone, beginning November 25, 1826, and continuing through April 1845.

Although none of the Mulkey brothers ever wrote for that publication, their names are mentioned in numerous communications regarding the religious activities among the preachers of the *Restoration Movement*.

Below are those activities of the Mulkeys, as they are revealed through various letters of correspondence.

The Mulkeys in the *Christian Messenger*

All three of the Mulkey brothers (John 1773-1845, Philip 1775-1844, and Isaac 1788-1855) are noted in the first volume of the *Christian Messenger* relating to the progress of the restored Gospel in Tennessee.

> The progress of liberal principles in Tennessee has been very far beyond our most sanguine anticipations. Its advocates have been opposed with all the might and ingenuity of man, aided by the popularity of their party, the long received dogmas of *orthodoxy*, and the furious zeal of bigotry. The more intelligent begin to see the weakness of their own arguments and aids to arrest the progress of these principles. One, a preacher of eminence in that country, lately in his address to a vast assembly, after having exhausted his store of arguments against those, who opposed the *orthodox* notions of

Trinity, of the Son of God, and of atonement, observed *that the civil authorities ought to interpose and put them down!* Some gentlemen of real republican principles, though not professors of religion, in disgust rose up and left the assembly. This information the Editor received while in that country, from a respectable source.

The brethren of the Christian name are not discouraged at this opposition, but zealously persevere in propagating what they deem to be the truth. They met in Conference, in August last, near Murfreesborough, and enjoyed a refreshing season from the presence of the Lord. About thirty believed and were baptized. The names of the Elders in that Conference are as follows:

John Bowman, Wm. Moore, Ephraim D. Moore, B. F. Hall, Wm. D. Jourdan, Abner Hill, James Y. Green, John Hooton, Francis A. Stone, Robert Randolph, Mansel W. Matthews, Wm. Clapp, Rob't Bates, Jno. Northcross, John O. Scott, Perius E. Harris, John M. Barnet, John Roberts, James E. Matthews, Crocket M'Donald, John M'Donald, Elisha Price, Elisha Randolph, Jno. Parkhill, Thacker Griffin, Lorenzo Griffin, Wm. D. Cams, Andrew Davis, John Green, Abner Peeler, **John Mulkey, Philip Mulkey**, Willis Hudleston, Wm. Gilbreath, Samuel D. Dewit, James Griffee, John M'Cartney, Robert Pedigo, Robert Leeper, — Stover, Elihu Randolph, **Isaac Mulkey**, Wm. Chaffin, — Johnson. The unordained preachers are, John Ward, Richard Lane, Calaway M'Gee, Henry Hays, &c.

The Churches in Tennessee and Alabama are numerous and fast increasing. We have recently received accounts from those countries, that at their meetings from 30 to 40 are frequently added to the Church. Many of the Elders are men of fine talents, of warm piety, and zeal, and are highly respected and beloved for their work's sake. May that unanimity and brotherly love, which have ever marked their course, still continue, to the glory of their Lord, and to the prosperity of Zion![2]

---

[2] Barton W. Stone, *Christian Messenger*, (November 25, 1826), Vol. 1, pp. 21-22.

Both John and Isaac are mentioned in the *Christian Messenger*, Volume 5, 1831; Philip Mulkey possibly having already gone to Franklin County, Illinois at this time, as noted in Chapter 3, page 41 of this book.

Extract of a letter from Elder James E. Matthews, to the Editor, dated:
Barton's, Ala. September 10th, 1831.

Br. Clough, - Yours of the 8th ult. came by last mail, at which time I was from home, attending a camp meeting. I now, in compliance with your request, hasten to reply, embracing the different subjects of enquiry contained in your letter.

With respect to the condition and prospects of the Christian churches in Alabama and Tennessee, I will state, that according to the best information which I have, there are about 60 churches in Tennessee, with probably 4000 members; and in Alabama, about 20 churches, with about 1500 members. Some of these churches are very large, and many of them are in a flourishing condition. When I came to this country, something over five years ago, there was one small church of about 10 members; that church now contains upward of 200 members, and I have planted another church in my immediate vicinity, of about 60 members. Elder Moore and myself have had great opposition by the popular sectaries, but that opposition has comparatively ceased. Our prospects, in one respect, are a little discouraging at present, as brother Moore is about to leave this country, and I am left with a broken constitution, and fast declining health, to attend to almost all of the churches in North Alabama.

There is one circumstance, in this country, which tends to check our progress. Our preachers have to rely almost entirely on the labor of their own hands for support. Many of the preachers are men of talents, and some of them of the first order, but few of them have engaged in writing. The doctrine of baptism "for the remission of sins," generally prevails, but in a more qualified sense than it is held by Alexander Campbell, editor of the Millennial Harbinger.

The following is a list of the names of most of the preachers in Tennessee and Alabama.

IN TENNESSEE - **John Mulkey, Isaac Mulkey**, Robert Randolph, Elihu Randolph, William D. Cams, Andrew Davis, Levi Nichols, Samuel Billingsley, William D. Jourdan, James Y. Green, Dr. — Becton, — Flinn, Levi Perkins, James Anderson, Corder Stone, John Hooton, William Hooton, — Bills, John M. Barnit, Edward Sweat, Andrew Carnachan, Mansel W. Matthews, Jessee Goodman, John Shultz, James Vinzant, Abner Hill, Henry Thompson, — Melvin, John M'Donald, Williams Nicks, and James Miller, (author of Trinitarianism unmasked.) John Green.

IN ALABAMA - James A. Anderson, Thacker Griffin, Lorenzo Griffin, Reuben Mardis: Jonathan Parker, William Price, Elisha Price, Ephraim D. Moore, — Crocket, — M'Donald, John Northcross, Jesse Wilks, Tolbert Fannin, Jonathan Wallis, Elisha Randolph, James E. Matthews.

The camp-meetings in this country, are now in progress. At four which have been holden, 45 have been immersed. The Alabama Conference commences in this country, on the last day of this month, and is regularly held, commencing on the Thursday before the first Lord's day in October, every year. We should rejoice to see some of our Northern brethren in the ministry among us.[3]

John and Isaac Mulkey attended the above-mentioned Alabama Conference, as indicated in Volume 6 of the *Christian Messenger*.

Religious Intelligence.

Bartons, Ala. Dec. 12, 1821

Dear Brother; - Our Conference commenced on the last day of Sept. During the meeting 19 persons were immersed, and a number more professed faith in Jesus; most of whom have been baptized since. In Limestone County 23 were immersed, and others confessed the Lord

---

[3] Barton W. Stone, *Christian Messenger*, (December 1831), Vol. 5, pp. 280-281.

Jesus. In Morgan Co. 4 were immersed; and in Blount county 8 were baptized, and several from the societies united with us.

At all the campmeetings [sic] in North Alabama, and in the South of Tennessee, about 176 persons put on the *Christian* [sic] *name* by immersion, and from the best information that I have received probably 130 more have been added to the churches since.

The following Elders were present at Conference, viz. **John Mulkey, Isaac Mulkey**, John Hooton, William Hooton, John M'Donald, Elisha Randolph, Eph. D. Moore, James Anderson, Tolbert Fannin, Mansel W. Matthews and myself.

In Conference, we dispensed with the etiquette usually observed. No bishop was called to the chair, nor was any clergyman or lay-member chosen President. We entered no resolves upon our minute book, nor did we take the name of an *"Advisory Council."* But "with one accord, in one place" we mutually engaged in arranging the appointments for our next annual meetings, so as to best promote the cause of the Redeemer; and agreed to request you to publish said Appointments in the Christian Messenger. *

Jas. E. Matthews.

*Camp meeting appointments deferred for next No. [4]

By 1832 we find through correspondence in the *Christian Messenger* that John Mulkey was back in Kentucky preaching.

Extract of a letter from Bishop A. Reynolds, dated, Glasgow, Sept. 28, 1832:

"ON LAST LORD'S DAY, I attended a meeting near Hopkinsville [a correction that appeared on page 352 of Volume 6 indicated that the

---

[4] Barton W. Stone, *Christian Messenger*, (January 1832), Vol. 6, pp. 26-27. The Camp Meeting Appointments were listed in Volume 6, No. 3, p. 94.

city was Tompkinsville instead of Hopkinsville], where I had the pleasure of meeting with my good old brother John Mulkey, &c. "We showed the utter insufficiency of all human contrivances to convert the world to God – and then presented the old Gospel, upon which seven confessed the Lord Jesus, six of whom were immersed into his name.

"Bro. Mulkey informed me that he had immersed some 20 or 30 for the remission of their sins, within a short time past," &c.[5]

On the facing page of that volume of the *Christian Messenger* is a letter from Elder W. D. Jourdan which gives an account of the work of the *Restoration* among the Baptists, and at the end of that correspondence, Jourdan updates his and John Mulkey's success and the great amount of labor that Mulkey was involved in at that time.

Elder W. D. Jourdan writes as follows:

Locust Shade, W. Tenn., Aug. 13, 1832.
Brethren Stone & Johnson: - Brother Jonathan H. Young, formally a *Baptist* preacher, but now a *Christian*, and engaged in the work of reformation, preached at our Meeting House, and staid [sic] all night with me, not long since, and desired me to give you the following account of his separation from the Baptist Church, which I promised to do:

"In August, 1829, I offered a letter, received from a Baptist Church in E. Tenn. to a Baptist Church on Wolf River, Overton county, W. Tenn., stating at the same time, to the Brethren, my objection to the *abstract of principles,* and that if they could receive me over the head of these things, I would be willing to live with them in peace; but if not, to return me my letter. And upon this ground they received me. We lived in harmony and peace until 1831, when some began to find fault of my preaching, saying that I indulged too far in the principle of reformation. I concluded to make an appointment, and give them my

---

[5] Barton W. Stone, *Christian Messenger*, (October 1832), Vol. 6, No. 10, p. 298.

views in full upon this subject; and accordingly did so. In consequence of this, Dr. I. Denton, pastor of the Clear Fork Church, Cumberland county, Ky., laid his grievance before this church against that on Wolf, for having received me over the head of the principles of the general union; and had members appointed to inquire of her whether guilty or not. She answered in the affirmative. They further inquired, do you intend to persist in this course? She said, she would answer no more inquiries, and the court then adjourned for a month, at which time, they returned again, making the same inquiries, their object being a negative answer, that I might be excluded and the church saved. But a majority stated that they make no further reply upon the subject. The proposition was then made, to ascertain who would stand upon the general principles of the union, and who would be in favor of the reformation. - The result was, a majority of one in favor of reformation. Then our separation took place. The minority then said, that those who remained under the covenant, composed the church, and pretended to exclude the majority. I proposed to Bro. Denton, to discuss the matter of difference between us, but he refused, saying, that these things had long since been decided.

"I now feel disposed to reform, where reformation is necessary, in myself, and to reform others as far as I can. May the Lord enable me to plead for the true reformation.

Yours in love,
J.H. Young."

Brothers - We have tolerably good times in our part. - On Sunday two weeks I immersed 6, and on the next Sunday 2 more. On the Tuesday evening following, Bro. Mulkey immersed 1. During our last meetings 4 have been reclaimed and 1 joined by letter, from the Baptist Church. The number of the church here is, at this time, 53. Bro. Mulkey rides nearly constantly, and is doing a great good - he appears to improve as fast, and faster, than some young men.

W.D. Jourdan[6]

---

[6] Barton W. Stone, *Christian Messenger*, (October 1832), Vol. 6, No. 10, pp. 299-300.

In 1833 correspondence we find that John Mulkey is again actively preaching back in Southern Kentucky at Burkesville.

> Brother Wm. D. Jourdan, of Tenn. writes, Sept. 7: - That brothers John Steele, John Mulkey and himself, held a 3 day's meeting at Burkesville, Ky., commencing 30th ult: - That 20 were joined to the church. On Saturday, and Lord's day before at Creelsburgh [Russell County, Kentucky], 19 were immersed. On Crocas Creek, on the way to Burkesville, 5 were immersed. Able teachers are greatly ueeded [needed].[7]

Immediately following is a letter to the same effect, although going into greater detail, from Pinckley W. Dryden.

> *Creelsborough Russell county, Ky. 23d Sept 1833.*
> Brother Stone:
> Knowing that you are at all times gratified at hearing of the success of the ancient gospel, I now take the liberty of informing you of its success in, and near this place.
> On Saturday and Sunday, the 24th and 25th days in August last, brother John Steele visited us, and before he left the neighbourhood [sic] 19 confessed and were immersed, for the remission of sins. The Friday, Saturday, and Lord's day following, brothers Steele, Jourdan and Mulkey, proclaimed the gospel at Burkesville, 22 there and the neighbourhood [sic], made the good confession and put on the Lord by immersion.
> Brother Steele and two others attended us again at this place yesterday and the day before, 26 more obeyed the Lord, and 19 Baptist Brethren came forward and united with us: the congregation at this place now numbers 34 members.
> When brother Steele visited us 4 weeks since, there were but 4 persons in the neighbourhood [sic] who believed in the doctrines of

---

[7] Barton W. Stone, *Christian Messenger*, (September 1833), Vol. 7, No. 9, p. 285.

the reformation. There was a large majority of those who confessed the Lord at this place, were young persons in the prime of life.

Yours, in hopes of perfect and eternal happiness beyond this world.

A. W. Stone.

Pinckney W. Dryden.[8]

Of particular interest is a letter under the head of "Religious Intelligence" in Volume 8, 1834 concerning the labors of Isaac Mulkey.

> Bro. Isaac Malkey [sic] of Roane co. E. Tenn. July 5. - Thus writes.
>
> I moved to this place 8 of 9 months ago. There were here 16 or 17, old disciples, who had been congregated 15 or 20 years ago by bro. E.D. Moore. Last Sept. we organised [sic] as nearly as we could with our knowledge on primitive grounds. On every first day we meet to break bread - we *attend* to the apostles doctrine, fellowship, and prayres [sic]. In November I had the pleasure of seeing one neighbor come and confess the Lord; and from that time we have enjoyed glorious refreshing seasons - Between 90 and 100 I have immersed.[9]

One reason the author draws attention to this letter is due to the fact that some Baptist historians claim that, while John and Philip Mulkey followed the reformation, their brother Isaac and their father Jonathan remained loyal to the Baptists.

Although John and Philip Mulkey deserted the Baptists, their father, Rev. Jonathan Mulkey, and their brother, Rev. Isaac Mulkey, remained faithful to the cause. Isaac Mulkey was a minister in the Buffalo Ridge Church as late as 1841, when he represented his home church as a delegate to the Holston Association.[10]

---

[8] Barton W. Stone, *Christian Messenger*, (September 1833), Vol. 7, No. 9, pp. 285-286.

[9] *Ibid*, (September 1834), Vol. 8, No. 9, p. 282.

[10] Cawthorn, Warnell, *Pioneer Baptist Church Records of South-Central Kentucky and the Upper Cumberland of Tennessee 1799-1899*, p. 438.

This author does not question whether Isaac Mulkey was represented as a delegate from the Buffalo Ridge Church in 1841, but from the correspondence of the *Christian Messenger* of September 1834, quoted above, it is obviously clear that Isaac Mulkey was conducting his efforts as a minister *"nearly as we could with our knowledge on primitive grounds,"* a clear indication that he, like his two older brothers, was actively involved in the reformation, at least at this point in his life.

Isaac Mulkey goes on to show that he had departed from Baptist practice in communion, as he indicated that the church he had organized in Roane County, East Tennessee, *"on every first day we meet to break bread."*

Observing communion every first day of the week was one of the things that separated the churches of the *Restoration* from the Baptists, and other denominations.

Even the minutes of the Mill Creek Baptist Church reveal that it was the custom of the Baptists to observe communion just three times a year.

> The church agree [sic] to commune 3 times in the year May, July and October.[11]

John Mulkey is again mentioned in Kentucky preaching in the year 1841.

In Volume 11 of the *Christian Messenger*, January 1841, there is a chart that gives a list of reporters and indicates the number of those that were added unto the Lord at various times during the preceding year, as well as the location where those additions took place.

John Mulkey is listed as one of the reporters from Kentucky, indicating that 90 had been added as of October 15, 1840.

---

[11] *Minutes of the Mill Creek Baptist Church*, (April 13, 1799), p. 11.

Reporters.	Location of Churches.	Dates.	No.
J T JOHNSON	PROVIDENCE; PARIS KY.	NOV 17	20
D P HENDERSON	LYNNVILLE, JACKSONVILLE, Ill.	do 11	43
J M MATHES	BLOOMINGTON LA.	do 5	13
M COMBS	AT VARIOUS POINTS IN LA.	do 5	75
JOHN SMITH	KY AND TEN.	do 7	89
W VANCE	COSHOCKTON, O.	do 3	8
J B NEW	AT VARIOUS POINTS IN LA.	do 11	117
J PHIIPS	GURSNSEY, MONROE O.	Oct 20	100
J M HARRIS	AT VARIOUS POINTS IN LA.	Sep.	23
E H SMITH	CROW'S CREE K KY. &C	Oct 8	23
JOHN MULKEY	KY.	do 15	90
T PITT	VARIOUS POINTS MO	do 10	48
J REED	REYNOLDSBURG, KENTON O.	do 12	6
G W M'REYNOLDS	MARTIN CO. LA.	Sept 27	15
C KENDRICK	ALA. AND TEN	Aug 20	181
T M ALLEN	VARIOUS POINTS IN MO.	do 20	74
J LOVELADY	PIATT CO. MO	do 20	11
J DOWLING	MARION CO. O.	Sept 15	50
B D CONAWAY	SOUTH RUN O	do 22	4
J CALAHAN	VARIOUS POINTS IN KY.	do 22	49
W S PATTERSON	VARIOUS POINTS IN OHIO	Aug 22	99
J A GANO	VARIOUS POINTS IN KY.	do 18	71
J BAUGH	VARIOUS POINTS IN Ill.	Oct 29	47
D DILLION	LEWIS CO. KY.	Nov 29	70
J B LUCAS	400 [sic]		---
		Total	1,720 [12]

The Mulkeys in Other Publications

The above chart from the *Christian Messenger* (1841) was very near the end of John Mulkey's active preaching career.

---

[12] Barton W. Stone, *Christian Messenger*, (January 1841), Vol. 11, p. 174.

In the August, 1845 *Millennial Harbinger*, Isaac T. Reneau wrote that John Mulkey gave up active preaching in about 1841, three years before his death. Reneau said that Mulkey delivered in 51 years over 10,000 sermons.

But we know that John Mulkey was active in both Kentucky and Tennessee in at least his last 20 years as a gospel preacher.

Writing concerning the history of the churches of the *Restoration Movement* in Tennessee, Earl Irving West says of John Mulkey:

> At least ten congregations were found in Jackson County before the war. The church at Liberty was organized by John Mulkey as early as 1826.[13]

West tells of John Mulkey baptizing W. C. Huffman in 1837 in Sumner County, Tennessee, Huffman going on to become a prominent preacher of the *Restoration.*

> The first congregation in Sumner County, Tennessee was organized by Sylvan Academy on March 30, 1834 by Professor Peter Hubbard. There were only nine members of the church. On the evening of April 22, 1837 W. C. Huffman was baptized here by John Mulkey.[14]

West also relates the story of how W. C. Huffman came to be baptized by Mulkey.

> Still another Tennessee preacher was W. C. Huffman. He was born of German parents in Central Kentucky on May 4, 1802. Early in his life he became a blacksmith. He had a powerful physical constitution and an extremely quick mind. Religiously, he was nothing in his early years. He reacted to the religious divisions by going into Universalism. He moved to Cairo, Tennessee on the Cumberland River in Sumner County in 1825. Two years later he married Lucy A Goodall, daughter

---

[13] Earl Irving West, *The Search for the Ancient Order*, Vol. 1, p. 252.
[14] *Ibid*, p.253.

of Charles Goodall. Meanwhile, he maintained his belief in Universalism until 1836 when he read the language of Jesus in Matt. 25:46. His father-in-law was a Cumberland Presbyterian. Huffman went to their meetings and turned away in disgust. He decided to study the Bible for himself to see if it were true. He concentrated upon the study of the Messiahship of Jesus. He concluded the Bible was true, and went back to the meetings determined to take nothing the preachers said unless it was read from the Bible. He went to the mourner's bench, but found no consolation for his soul. At night, he couldn't sleep. Once he got up, put on a light, and read his Bible, and resolved to be immersed. The next morning early he went to an old man by the name of Wiseman, a Baptist preacher. The preacher asked Huffman for a personal experience, so it could be told to the church the next Sunday, but Huffman insisted that he wanted to be baptized for the remission of his sins. Wiseman refused but told Huffman that a man would be preaching that kind of doctrine the next week at Peter Hubbard's school house. Huffman went and heard John Mulkey. He was immersed on April 22, 1837. Huffman labored with the churches in Sumner County until after the war. The last two years of his life he preached at Union City in West Tennessee, he died on February 19, 1880.[15]

But the efforts of the Mulkeys were not just confined to the fields of Kentucky and Tennessee.

Philip Mulkey wrote a report of his efforts in Franklin County, Illinois to the *Millennial Harbinger* on June 7, 1839 and noted:

> Our little congregation keeps growing in numbers. A little over three years ago we numbered 20. The present number I cannot tell correctly; but suppose there are about 90. Some have come forward

---

[15] Earl Irving West, *The Search for the Ancient Order*, Vol. 1, p. 256-257; also see A. Alsup, "Wilkinson C. Huffman," *Gospel Advocate*, Vol. 22, No. 21 (May 20, 1880), pp. 328-329.

at almost every meeting lately and publicly made the good confession...

Earl Irving West, in his biography of Elder Ben Franklin and his labors in Indiana, credited John Mulkey as being one of the first preachers of the *Restoration* in that state.

> In years to come the memories of Indiana Christians and of Bethel, in particular, lingered with him [Ben Franklin]. When moving there in 1843, Franklin was aware that this was one of the first congregations to be planted in the state. Here, John Mulkey, Barton W. Stone and David Purviance had preached the primitive gospel, and he felt honored to work where they had once served Christ...[16]

As we close this chapter, it's easy to see from the above documents that John, Philip, and Isaac Mulkey were all actively involved in spreading New Testament Christianity, not only in the Mill Creek area, but throughout Southern Kentucky and Northern Tennessee; even as far north as Illinois and Indiana.

From some of the correspondence, we were also introduced to some the preachers that worked alongside the Mulkeys, and were able to pick up a few hints as to how the doctrines that they were preaching differed from the Baptists, from which they parted fellowship.

In our next chapter we will look at a few of the men closely associated with the Mulkeys, and reveal even further proof that *Restoration* message of these men was heading away from denominationalism, and back toward the *Ancient Order of Things*.

---

[16] Earl Irving West, *Elder Ben Franklin: Eye of the Storm*, P.33.

A History of the Mill Creek ("Old Mulkey") Church
Tompkinsville, Kentucky

Chapter 7

The State of the Restoration
(Through the Writings of Mulkey's Associates)

Although John, Philip, and Isaac Mulkey weren't actively involved as writers for religious periodicals, we were able in our last chapter to become acquainted with some of the other *Restoration* preachers that worked closely with the Mulkeys.

As a result, we are able to look at the events that those associates wrote about, and not only get an idea of the atmosphere of the times, but by logical deduction, also ascertain the conditions under which the Mulkey brothers labored, as well as some of the principles for which they contended.

Alexander Reynolds

In our previous chapter, page 101, we included a letter by Alexander Reynolds of Glasgow, dated September 28, 1832, which indicated that he held a meeting near Tompkinsville with John Mulkey within the past week.

In that letter Reynolds said concerning the meeting:

..."We showed the utter insufficiency of all human contrivances to convert the world to God - and then presented the old Gospel, upon which seven confessed the Lord Jesus, six of whom were immersed into his name.

"Bro. Mulkey informed me that he had immersed some 20 or 30 for the remission of their sins, within a short time past," &c. [1]

Taking those comments at face value, we can logically assume that Mulkey and Reynolds were contending for the same religious principles.

Having come to that conclusion, we can look at another letter that Reynolds wrote, dated just 10 days earlier (September 18, 1832) and get some indication of what conditions the two men were laboring under, seeing that both Mulkey and Reynolds had at one time been connected with the Green River Association, but had since parted fellowship with that Baptist organization.

Glasgow, Ky. Sept. 18, 1832.

The Green River united Baptist Association.

Brother Johnson. - As I am persuaded that a knowledge of the existing state of things in this Association would interest your readers, I have concluded to state a few facts, which, if you think proper you may insert in the Messenger.

Some three or four years ago, some of us, having been enabled to discriminate between the pure and simple gospel of Christ and the traditions of men which have long intercepted the light of Heaven, determined to renounce the latter and sustain the former. No sooner had this determination been announced than the mournful cry of heresy was heard in every direction. We told our brethren not to be alarmed: that we intended to renounce only what was purely traditional, and adhere closely to that faith and those forms of worship taught by Christ and the holy twelve. But they took the attachment we manifested for the word of God alone, to be certain evidence that we were Campbellites. They divided several churches; - the minorities claiming the constitution, excluding the majorities. This state of things, however, had not long existed until the Association undertook to heal the abounding divisions. It, with Elder Jacob Lock at its head, sustained us and rejected the minorities who had excluded

---

[1] Barton W. Stone, *Christian Messenger*, (October 1832), Vol. 6, No. 10, p. 298.

us. They (the minorities of the divided churches, about 4 or 5 in number,) formed themselves into an organized body and claimed to be the Green River Association. They have for their leader, Elder Ralph Petty. Last year, they declared the whole Association from which they withdrew to be Campbellites. Since that time, their body has increased considerably; and that too, at the expense of Elder Lock and his party, for as one increases the other must decrease.

Elder Lock and his folks, seeing that the minority of the Association, by urging their claims to the general union, succeeded last year in getting into, or rather keeping in correspondence with the surrounding Associations, and feeling the loss of popularity abroad, determined to make a vigorous effort to regain their (his) standing. Seeing how the game was going, they all of a sudden became exceedingly orthodox, though Elder Lock and others had made considerable advances toward reformation. They commenced shutting down meeting-house doors, proscribing [sic] and persecuting us most violently. At their Association this year, they proposed uniting again with the minority; but the minority, not having as much confidence in them as perhaps they would, if they had not seen them persecute the very cause and the very people that they once labored to sustain, rejected their proposition. They then excluded 3 or 4 churches, and took two or three more under dealings. In their Minutes I see that those of us who have acted anything like a prominent part in the reformation are accused of deceitfulness, which we repel as a malicious slander and challenge them to proof. They next say "that we endeavor to conceal our real sentiments, and yet exert ourselves in spreading the contagion." Now if they can tell how a man can conceal his sentiments and at the same time spread them, I will never charge them with asserting a falsehood.

To look at the hostile attitude in which the two Associations now stand toward each other, and toward those who acknowledge the gospel alone, it would seem that they were fighting about mere differences of opinion as to the best way to kill what they call Campbellites. But no doubt, the chief cause of the war is, who shall have the best reputation tor orthodoxy?

Having briefly stated the conditions of the Association, I will now say a word or two in regard to our own condition. We now have seven congregations who have dissolved all connexion [sic] with the Association, and 2 or 3 more I think, will soon make their escape without the smell of fire upon their garments. We are out of the confusion, the war going on among the Babylonians themselves. Upon the whole, the old gospel is gaining ground: every few weeks some confess the Lord. In the course of this year some 20 or 30 have been immersed into the name of the Lord Jesus.

As a specimen of the kind of opposition made against us, I will give the following charges, upon which I was excluded by the minority of the Smith's Grove [Kentucky] Church, which now forms a part of the Petty Association. I present them to you just as they have published them in their minutes and in the newspaper published at Bowling Green:

"Whereas the church is unhappily involved in divisions, feelings and sentiments, by A. Reynolds preaching or teaching doctrines not contained in the holy scriptures.

1. Whereas the said Reynolds has openly opposed the constitution or articles of faith or agreement in which we stand united, and under which he said Reynolds was received into this church, by calling it a human creed, without attempting to prove it to be *human laws* and not *divine laws*, and refusing to be governed by it.

2. For privately asking members of this church if they could or would not put down the creed or constitution of this church, and take the New Testament for their creed, telling at the same time it was their own ignorance alone that prevented their understanding the New Testament, for that there was nothing dark or mysterious in it to him, thereby conveying the idea that it was fully in the natural power of each individual to understand it perfectly; all of which we believe calculated to gender strife and confusion, and contrary to the doctrines contained in the Holy Writ.

3. For attempting to erase from the mind of the creature man every view and light that he or they have of experimental religion, by doing away [with] experience, by saying that the mind cannot stand still and

when it gets in trouble about something it increases till it gets to the highest pitch it can bear, and as it cannot stand on that point it turns and receives some relief, or ease, and some gladness, from that into joy, and then it is that the creature man thinks that he is converted from darkness to the marvelous light of Christ; but he, the said Reynolds cried out with uplifted hands, and said, it is imagination, ideal, and all delusion of the mind.

4. For saying that the Holy Spirit does not teach the mind to pray or preach, thereby conveying the idea that the work is alone of man, and not by the divine influence of the Holy Spirit, on the mind.

5. For conveying the idea that the Holy Spirit does not operate on, and influence the mind of the lay members or man in general, by asking the questions, how did it feel? how did it look? what did it say to you? did it speak in an audible voice? or in what way did it operate on you?

6. For saying or advising in the pulpit, to come out from popery and all creeds, thus breeding discord and confusion in the church.

7. For saying to a member of this church that he, the said Reynolds, knew nothing about natural or spiritual quickening.

8. For saying in the pulpit that a man has the same power to believe that he has to disbelieve; thereby conveying the idea, that there is no need of the Holy Spirit to lead a soul from darkness to light."

But very few of these charges are stated in my own words. It is true, however, that I did, and do yet advise all men to come out from popery and all *human* creeds, and take the New Testament for their creed. This I acknowledge to be divine. But because I was not so eagle-eyed as to see divinity in their little man-made laws, I was treated by them as a heathen and a publican. Several other things stated are true; but some are only partially true. In relation to the 7th charge, I have only to say that an old man a little suspicious of my orthodoxy, did ask me, in the presence of a company of ladies, what I thought of natural quickening, and to avoid discussion of the subject at that time, I was forced to tell him that I knew little or nothing about it. But whether or not I deserved exclusion from the church on account of what is here laid to my charge, I leave the world to judge. Wishing you great success in extending the knowledge of the truth, I subscribe myself your brother in Christ,

ALEXANDER REYNOLDS.[2]

Much indeed is learned from the above letter, not only about what subjects Mulkey and Reynolds might have preached at their meeting near Tompkinsville, but also the general reaction of the Baptists concerning those subjects.

Like John Mulkey, Alexander Reynolds was also personally acquainted with Barton W. Stone and was aware of the principles for which Stone contended.

Mulkey had become friends with Stone in 1801 when he attended Stone's Cane Ridge Revival with David Haggard of Burkesville. Reynolds had met Stone in 1832 when Stone had stopped and preached at Glasgow, Kentucky while on his way to Tennessee.

The following letter by Reynolds to associate editor of the *Christian Messenger*, J. T. Johnson, tells of that visit and the impression Stone made upon Reynolds, and also gives us another glimpse of the difficulties that Mulkey, Stone, and Reynolds labored under during this period.

Glasgow, Ky. June 4th, 1832.

Brother Johnson - Since Bro. Davis has been in Georgetown I have received several numbers of the Christian Messenger, and am pleased with the intelligence it brings.

A short time ago old Bro. Stone staid [sic] one night in our town, on his way to Tennessee, and addressed us publicly, on the subject of Christ's receiving sinners. After hearing him, and conversing with him on different topics, as well as on some local matters, I was forced to the conclusion, that no man was ever more unjustly persecuted and set at naught, by the worshippers of sectarian orthodoxy, than he.

When I see such men denounced as heretics, for no other cause than, conscientiously believing what our Heavenly Father has said, and zealously obeying what he has *commanded*, I am the more willing to suffer all the hard censures, misrepresentations, and persecutions of

---

[2] *Christian Messenger*, (October 1832), Vol. 6, No. 10, pp. 303-306.

those, who either ignorantly, or willfully oppose the truth. The Gospel requires, that in meekness, we should suffer all, though their abuses, in some instances, would well nigh extinguish the patience of Job, and exhort the curse of Balaam.

Your neighbor, Chambers, in his last Chronicle, has announced the decline, and in some places the *death*, of what he is pleased to call Campbellism. If his meaning be, that those who have renounced the traditions of men, and taken the word of God for their only guide in all matters of faith and obedience, are Campbellites, or the followers of any man, his assertions should be regarded in no other light than a malicious slander. He well knows, that we profess to follow Christ *only*; and, for one, I defy him, in all we believe and teach, to show one single departure from the Gospel. Neither is the truth, which he nicknames Campbellism, palsied by his efforts to keep the public ignorant of its progress. It is mighty and still prevails. There are six or eight churches in Barren and Warren counties, that acknowledge the right of Zion's glorious King to rule; and every one will be deceived, if more are not shortly built, "upon the foundation of the Prophets and Apostles, Jesus being the Chief corner stone."

In the same piece, he represents us as having united with Arians; and consequently, as having embraced the peculiar notions of those, on whom he would cast an odium, by applying to them an opprobrious name. It is possible that he has yet to learn that we have not united, neither intend to unite, upon any of the *Unitarian* or *Trinitarian* speculations. As far as I am acquainted with the Christian brethren, they all seem to be content with the belief of the great fact that, "Jesus is the Son of God," without any useless speculation about the particular *sense* in which he is God's Son. But upon an agreement to take the word of God for our *only* guide, and speak of the Son of God as the New Testament writers have spoken of him, a union has commenced between us, which I do hope, will extend till all who love Jesus will become one in him.

When will the man of sin cease to reign? When will divisions be healed? When will angry feelings, bitter strifes, and fierce contentions, the offspring of corruption, be banished to their native region of darkness? O! when will the scattered sheep of Christ be gathered into one fold? Will the silken cords of that love that induced Jesus to come down and die, ever bind this jarring world together? Yes, the word of truth assures us that it is still efficacious. Our labor to build up Zion is then not in vain in the Lord. My dear Brother; I am happy to see you successfully engaged in this good work - a work which God will own and bless, when a mother's love shall cease towards the child she bears. You may think me enthusiastical; but I have great confidence in the success of truth, and the universal enjoyment of all its gracious influences.

Your brother in hope of glory.

ALEXANDER REYNOLDS.[3]

Prior to his adoption of the *Restoration* principles, Alexander Reynolds had been an active Baptist.

He was one of the charter members of the Boiling Springs Baptist Church in Hart County, Kentucky when it was formed as a daughter of the Green River Baptist Church in 1825.

Boiling Springs Baptist Church appears to be a daughter of the Green River Baptist Church. A group of Christians "met at the home of Dudley Roundtree on Spring Creek (Boiling Springs) on the second Saturday in July 1825. Brother Johnston Graham from Brush Creek Church; Brother Thomas Whitman from South Fork of Nolin Church; and Brothers James Wilson, Alexander Reynolds, and William Whitman from Green River Church were received by those from Spring Creek who wished to form a church. A presbytery was formed and Boiling Springs Church came into being."[4]

---

[3] *Christian Messenger*, (July 1832), Vol. 6, No. 7, pp. 217-218.

[4] Cawthorn, Warnell, *Pioneer Baptist Church Records of South-Central Kentucky and the Upper Cumberland of Tennessee 1799-1899*, p. 177.

Reynolds had been a messenger to the Green River Baptist Association from the Green River Church in Hart County, Kentucky in 1824 and 1826.[5]

He was also a messenger to that same Association from the Smith's Grove Baptist Church in Warren County, Kentucky four straight years, 1827-1830.[6]

His name was also listed in the constitution of the Cedar Springs Baptist Church of Edmonson County, Kentucky in 1829:

The constitution of Cedar Spring United Baptist Church

"The United Baptist Church of Christ was constituted and called Cedar Spring on the 28th of November 1829 by Elder James Mitchell and Alexander Reynolds...

Elder Alexander Reynolds, a minister in the presbytery, was a member of old Green River Church at Munfordsville. He was ordained by Green River Church on the fourth Saturday in June 1824 by Brethren Ralph Petty, S.M. Bagby, John Davidson and William Whitman.[7]

He also helped constitute the Brownsville Baptist Church in Edmonson County, Kentucky in June 1829.[8]

In view of the above information, it is easy to see that Alexander Reynolds and John Mulkey had very much in common. Both had been very active in Baptist affairs and had helped establish many churches for that cause in Southern Kentucky. It is easy to see why both came under such severe persecution of tongue by the Baptists after they withdrew from that organization and adopted the principles of New Testament Christianity.

"Raccoon" John Smith

John Mulkey was also acquainted with "Raccoon" John Smith, one of the most colorful, and prominent preachers of the *Restoration Movement.*

---

[5] *Pioneer Baptist Church Records of South-Central Kentucky and the Upper Cumberland of Tennessee 1799-1899*, p. 185.

[6] *Ibid*, p. 247.

[7] *Ibid*, p. 278.

[8] *Ibid*, p. 300.

(John) Mulkey was a friend of both "Raccoon" John Smith and Barton W. Stone. Having lived in the same neighborhood with John Smith in Tennessee, Mulkey invited Smith on several occasions to preach at what was now becoming known as the "Mulkey Meeting House." On October 10, 1817, Stone wrote Mulkey asking him to come to Cane Ridge for a communion service. Considering the distance and the fact that the trip would be made on horse back [sic], this was more than a casual invitation from one preacher to another. Stone concludes by writing, "...my love to you remains unabated."[9]

Like Mulkey, Smith had once been associated with the Baptists, his family being charter members in the formation of the Clear Fork Baptist Church (Stockton Valley No 2) in Clinton County, Kentucky. His father, George Smith, is listed in the original constitution of that church.

The names of those who entered the constitution of Clear Fork Church on April 1, 1802, are: Isaac Denton, George Smith, Wm. Wood, Thos. Stockton, Samuel Wood, Wm Goodson, Sr., James Crouch, Anna Denton, Sr., Agness Crouch, Benj. Campbell, Clea Campbell, Jame Brock Sr., Martha Denton.[10]

After departing from the Baptists, Smith moved to North- Central Kentucky where he was closely associated with Barton W. Stone, Alexander Campbell, John Rogers, J. T. Johnson, and numerous other influential preachers of the *Restoration.*

After the union of the *"Christians"* (those connected with Barton W. Stone) and the "Reformers" (those associated with Alexander Campbell) in Kentucky in January 1832, "Raccoon" John Smith and John Rogers were selected as evangelists and sent to visit churches throughout the South.

---

[9] E. Clayton Gooden, January, 1965 issue of the *Discipliana*, reprinted in The Kentucky Explorer, February, 1993, p. 27.

[10] *Pioneer Baptist Church Records of South-Central Kentucky and the Upper Cumberland of Tennessee 1799-1899*, p. 482.

In order to consummate the union, John Smith and John Rogers were requested, after due conference among the Elders and brethren, to visit all the churches of Kentucky; and the arrangement was announced in the [*Christian*] *Messenger* of January, 1832, in the following words:

"To increase and consolidate this union, and to convince all our sincerity, we, the Elders and brethren, have separated two Elders, John Smith and John Rogers, the first known *formally* by the name Reformer, the latter by the name Christian. These brethren are to ride together through all the churches, and be equally supported by the united contributions of the churches of both descriptions; which contributions are to be deposited together, with Brother John T. Johnson as treasurer and distributor."[11]

According to E. Clayton Gooden (page 119 of this book), "Raccoon" John Smith often visited and preached at the Mill Creek Church and was closely associated with John Mulkey for a number of years.

Smith wrote to the *Christian Messenger* of one such visit to Southern Kentucky.

Extract from a letter of Eld. Jno. Smith.
Mountsterling, Ky. August 22, 1834.

Bro. J. T. Johnson,

A few days since, I returned home from a tour of 32 days length. In which time I passed through several counties in the State as far down as Wayne, and Cumberland. Thence through 6 or 7 counties in Tennessee. Thence into Madison co. Alabama. I can assure you that the Christians in this section of the country, see but a small corner of the field, which *loudly, loudly*, calls for laborers. In those parts, through which I have recently traveled, there are thousands of people who never have heard the gospel proclaimed in its primitive purity, and simplicity. The sects are completely buried in the rubbish of their own traditions; and sinners do not know what they must do to be

---

[11] John A. Williams, *Life of Elder John Smith*, pp. 458-459.

saved, and (in many -- very many places) there is no one to tell them. Hundreds are begging for some one [sic] to visit them. I did not remain long enough at any one place to deliver more than one discourse except in two cases; and of course had not an opportunity of gathering much fruit. Notwithstanding all the disadvantages, 35 made the good confession in my tour. If you wish to see a complete and moral waste, take a journey through that part of the country; and I think your spirit will be stirred within you, to see the people wholly given to sectarianism. Still the prospects for doing good are abundant and flattering. The great body of the people would hear and obey, if they had the opportunity.[12]

The sad indications of this letter not only reveal the tremendous work load that was placed upon the shoulders of John Mulkey and the few preachers for the primitive cause that resided and worked in Southern Kentucky and Northern Tennessee, but also serves to illustrate why we see John Mulkey's name appearing in so many different localities during his ministry.

The harvest was plentiful, but the laborers were few.

We can perhaps learn something more of John Mulkey's religious sentiments during this period by reading the writings of his close associate John Smith.

In his biography by John A. Williams, Smith gives his reasons for departing from the Baptist faith.

I have sometimes been asked why I left the Baptist Church, and I have, on several occasions, answered, in substance, as follows:

I. I did not believe the doctrines of the Philadelphia Confession of Faith to be in accordance with the Word of God; and, of course, I could not conscientiously teach them.

II. I could not find such a thing as a *Baptist Church* named in the Bible.

III. I found that the kind of experience which they required was unknown to any of the saints of the New Testament. I recalled my own

---

[12] *Christian Messenger*, (October 1834), Vol. 8, No. 10, p. 316.

experience, and compared it with other conversions given in the Bible; and I was astonished to find that sinners, when convicted of sin and desired salvation, instead of agonizing for months, as I had done, did not wait a single day to find it; except, perhaps, Saul of Tarsus, who waited and prayed three days before he was told what to do. In bringing every thing [sic] to test, however, I found these points in my experience:

1. I believed sincerely in the Lord Jesus; this I knew the Word of God required, and I felt conscious of this qualification.

2. I was conscious that I had repented of all of my sins; this, also, I knew the Word of God demanded.

3. I knew that I had been immersed; and this, I saw, the Lord required of every believing penitent.

I saw clearly that instead of being required to tell all the workings of my mind, they should have required these three things and nothing more, in order to my admission into the Church. True, when I was immersed, I submitted to it simply as a command of God, without knowing the blessings connected with it.

IV. I found, also, this glaring inconsistency among the Baptists: while they taught that a man must be a Christian in the Bible sense of that term, before they could admit him to baptism, yet, until he was baptized, they allowed him no more privileges among them than a pagan or a publican.

V. I was well persuaded that God never authorized any man or set of men to make Articles of Faith or Rules of Practice for the subjects of his kingdom.

VI. I was convinced, moreover, that it was not the custom of the ancient and apostolic churches to eat the Lord's Supper, monthly, or quarterly, but that the disciples met together for that purpose every first day of the week.

Now, convinced as I was that the Baptists taught many erroneous, and some dangerous, doctrines - that they had given their church a name unauthorized by the Scriptures - that their practice of admitting members to baptism by *experience* was also unauthorized - that they assumed the authority to make laws and rules for the government of

Christ's Church - that they neglected to celebrate the Lord's death more than two, four, or twelve times a year; seeing all these things, I could not conscientiously remain a Baptist, *especially when they were not willing for me to preach and practice among them what I believed to be the truth.*[13]

"Raccoon" John Smith is probably best remembered for the address that he gave in January 1832 at the union of the *"Christians"* and the *"Reformers"* at Lexington, Kentucky.

It reveals something of his character, and the cause to which he, Mulkey, and others dedicated their lives.

> God has but one people on the earth. He has given to them but one Book, and therein exhorts and commands them to be one family. A union, such as we plead for - a union of God's people on that one Book - must, then, be practicable.
>
> Every Christian desires to stand complete in the whole will of God. The prayer of the Savior, and the whole tenor of his teachings, clearly show that it is God's will that his children should be united. To the Christian, such a union must be desirable.
>
> But an amalgamation of sects is not such a union as Christ prayed for, and God enjoins. To agree to be one upon any system of human invention would be contrary to his will, and could never be a blessing to the Church or the world; therefore the only union practicable or desirable must be based on the Word of God, as the only rule of faith and practice.
>
> There are certain abstruse or speculative matters - such as the mode of the *Divine Existence*, and the *Ground and Nature of the Atonement* - that have, for centuries, been themes of discussion among Christians. These questions are as far from being settled now as they were in the beginning of the controversy. By a needless and intemperate discussion of them much feeling has been provoked, and divisions have been produced.

---

[13] John A. Williams, *Life of Elder John Smith*, pp. 293-295.

For several years past I have tried to speak on such subjects only in the language of inspiration; for it can offend no one to say about those things just what the Lord himself has said. In this scriptural style of speech all Christians should be agreed. It can not [sic] be wrong - it can do no harm. If I come to the passage, "My Father is greater than I," I will quote it, but will not stop to speculate upon the inferiority of the Son. If I read, "Being in the form of God, he thought it not robbery to be equal with God," I will not stop and speculate upon the consubstantial nature of the Father and Son. I will not linger to build a theory on such texts, and thus encourage a speculative and wrangling spirit among my brethren. I will present these subjects only in the words which the Lord has given to me. I know he will not be displeased if we say just what he has said. Whatever opinions about these and similar subjects I may have reached, in the course of my investigations, if I never distract the church of God with them, or seek to impose them on my brethren, they will never do the world any harm.

I have the more cheerfully resolved on this course, because the Gospel is a system of facts, commands, and promises, and no deduction or inference from them, however logical or true, forms any part of the Gospel of Jesus Christ. No heaven is promised to those who hold them, and no hell is threatened to those who deny them. They do not constitute, singly or together, any item of the ancient apostolic Gospel.

While there is but one faith, there may be ten thousand opinions; and hence, if Christians are ever to be one, they must be in one faith, and not in opinion. When certain subjects arise, even in conversation or social discussion, about which there is a contrariety of opinion and sensitiveness of feeling, speak of them in the words of the Scriptures, and no offense will be given, and no pride of doctrine will be encouraged. We may even come, in the end, by thus speaking the same things, to think the same things.

For several years past, I have stood pledged to meet the religious world, or any part of it, on the ancient Gospel and order of things, as presented in the words of the Book. This is the foundation on which

Christians once stood, and on it they can, and ought to, stand again. From this I can not [sic] depart to meet any man, or set of men, in the wide world. While, for the sake of peace and Christian union, I have long since waived the public maintenance of any speculation I may hold, yet *not one Gospel fact, commandment, or promise, will I surrender for the world!*

Let us, then, brethren, be no longer Campbellites or Stonites, New Lights or Old Lights, or any other kind of *lights*, but let us all come to the Bible, and to the Bible alone, as the only book in the world that can give us all the Light we need.[14]

The events that Alexander Reynolds and John Smith wrote of, for the most part, were concerning the conflicts that the reformation had among the Baptists. But there were other denominations that John Mulkey and the preachers associated with him had to face on similar grounds.

W.D. Jourdan

In our previous chapter (page 102) W. D. Jourdan, writing from Locust Shade, west Tennessee, describes the success that he and John Mulkey had in their meetings of October, 1832.

> *Brothers* - We have tolerably good times in our part. - On Sunday two weeks I immersed 6, and on the next Sunday 2 more. On the Tuesday evening following, Bro. Mulkey immersed 1. During our last meetings 4 have been reclaimed and 1 joined by letter, from the Baptist Church. The number of the church here is, at this time, 53. Bro. Mulkey rides nearly constantly, and is doing a great good - he appears to improve as fast, and faster, than some young men.
>
> W.D. Jourdan[15]

Then, in a letter of correspondence to the *Christian Messenger* in 1833 he tells of their success in meetings in and around Burkesville, Kentucky.

---

[14] *Life of Elder John Smith*, pp. 452-454.
[15] *Christian Messenger*, (October 1832), Vol. 6, No. 10, pp. 299-300.

Brother Wm. D. Jourdan, of Tenn. writes, Sept. 7: - That brothers John Steele, John Mulkey and himself, held a 3 day's meeting at Burkesville, Ky., commencing 30th ult: - That 20 were joined to the church. On Saturday, and Lord's day before at Creelsburgh [Russell County, Kentucky], 19 were immersed. On Crocas Creek, on the way to Burkesville, 5 were immersed. Able teachers are greatly ueeded [needed].[16]

In a report concerning statistical information reported from Kentucky churches in a letter that was dated June 25, 1831 by John Jones, Jr., Wm. D. Jourdan was the reporter for the churches near the Kentucky-Tennessee line.

Jourdan reported that the Burkesville Church in Cumberland County, Kentucky, established in 1829, had a membership of 14. At the Cumberland Meeting-House, planted in 1828, there were 68 members. The Crocus Creek Church, also in Cumberland County, consisted of 20 members. Jourdan also reported that the Overton Church, in Overton County, Tennessee, planted in 1830, had a membership of 22.

Of particular interest in regard to William D. Jourdan is a debate that he held in Cumberland County with a Methodist preacher by the name of J. Stamper.

The notice of the debate appeared in the March 1829 issue of the *Christian Messenger*.

NOTICE - *For the Christian Messenger.*
On the 8th of April next, at 9 o'clock, A. M., a debate between J. Stamper, Presiding Elder in the Methodist Church, and W. D. Jourdan, a member of the Church of Christ, will be opened. The proposition to be discussed is - *Jesus Christ is the very and Eternal God*. The seat of action is Marrowbone Meeting House, Cumberland County, Ky. Mr. J Stamper takes the affirmative, and Mr. Jourdan the negative of this proposition. It is to continue three days, if no more; neither to exceed one hour in any one speech.

---

[16] *Christian Messenger*, (September 1833), Vol. 7, No. 9, p. 285.

INFORMANT.[17]

The results of that debate also appeared in the *Christian Messenger*, in a release dated April 8, 1830.

(COMMUNICATED.)
Cumberland County, Ky. March 8, 1830.

Mr. Stone - At this late period, I will give you an account of the debate of April last, between Messrs. Stamper and Jourdan.

This I am compelled to do, by the false reports now in circulation, not in this country, but at a distance; which are prejudicial in their nature to Truth. However, I may not recollect every thing that might be necessary to this publication: Yet, as I live in the county where it was held, I cannot fail in giving the truth, with regard to the general opinion respecting that debate: which is, that Mr. Jourdan had decidedly the advantage in point of argument. But it may be necessary, owing to some reports, to relate the circumstances which gave rise to this debate. This I shall do to the best information I have.

Near the close of 1828, Mr. Dungan, a Methodist preacher, preached on Crocus Creek in this county; and after preaching, in conversation with some gentlemen, said that he would discuss the Divinity of Jesus Christ with Mr. Jourdan, or find a man to do it. Mr. Jourdan on hearing this, wrote Mr. Dungan a friendly challenge; giving him the privilege, should he decline the invitation, to fill his place with the man of his choice - he declined, and Mr. Stamper took his place, and wrote to Mr. Jourdan his acceptance of the challenge. Soon after they met in Burkesville, and in the presence of Messrs. Saufley, Owsly and Taylor, agreed upon a time, place, and some other preliminaries. These are the circumstances that gave rise to the debate, as near as I can recollect. On Wednesday the 8th they met, but the day was spent in deciding upon the third Moderator, and the opening of the *debate*. It was finally agreed, that Dr. Joel Owsley should serve, and that Mr. Stamper should open and conclude with a half hour each. Never did I

---

[17] *Christian Messenger*, (March 29), Vol. 3, No. 5, p. 119.

see a set of Clergymen, so highly impregnated with the hope of victory, as Mr. Stamper and his brethren appeared to be, at the commencement of the debate. But it was manifest to many during the first intermission, that their hope of victory was on the decline; and about the close of that day, great discouragement appeared among them. And before the close of the debate hope seemed entirely to disappear. But to return - We were then dismissed to meet next morning at 9 o'clock. About the time appointed the parties arrived, and a considerable multitude. Mr. Stamper began, directly introducing Arians and Socinians, alleging that all anti-Trinitarians properly belonged to one or the other of those systems. And after making some quotations in his favor (as he supposed,) his time expired. Mr. Jourdan, then arose and observed to the people, that he wished them to understand distinctly, that he stood on the negative side of the proposition; & that his opponent was bound on the affirmative, according to their preliminaries.

He also, remarked to them, that the trinity was not the subject of discussion, as his opponent had insinuated, but that it was, whether *Jesus Christ was the very and Eternal God* or not. He then attended to his quotations and arguments, particularly answering him where there was any necessity.

Mr. Stamper arose, and read the challenge to Mr. Dungan, thereby endeavoring to prove that Mr. Jourdan was equally bound on the affirmative as himself; although, he had consented in the preliminaries that he should stand on the negative. He then, from some cause or other, was induced to call for two gentlemen to read for him - this, Mr. Jourdan could have prevented, but he chose not to do it, bnt [but] to let Mr. Stamper go on under this dishonor. One of these gentlemen stood on his right, the other on his left hand - the latter being a Greek scholar frequently expounded for him. One used the Old, the other the New Testament reading of his citations as he directed them from his note book. Mr. Jourdan was asked by some of his friends, if he would call for help also, he observed that he would if his cause was a bad one, but as it was a good one, he had no need of any aid except that of his Bible. Mr. Jourdan began, by expressing his sorrow that Mr.

Stamper had still refused to answer his questions, or even to examine his quotations; he again, solicited him to respond like a man when he arose, and not keep himself at a distance, but to come in close grips, that the contest might be ended. But all this was to no effect; for when Mr. Stamper arose he pursued his former course, not at all responding. The evening arrived, and we were dismissed to meet at 9 o'clock next morning.

Next morning, before the debate began, Mr. Stamper's Moderator made application to Mr. Jourdan, for the debate to come to a close; and that the time must be set. Mr. Jourdan observed, that he and Mr. Stamper had limited the time to three days, and that it was not his province to interfere with this arrangement. Mr. Linsey again said, that it must come to a close. Mr. Jourdan replied that he would do nothing in the matter then, and so they went into the debate. In the first speech by Mr. Jourdan, he presented to Mr. Stamper about thirty written questions, which he had prepared the night before; and personally requested him to answer them, or to acknowledge that he could not, and then he would ask him no more. When Mr. Stamper arose, he just observed, I arise to prosecute the subject, and do not feel myself bound to answer his catalogue of questions. Nor did he so much as ever name one of them.

At twelve, during the intermission, Mr. Linsey resumed his application to Mr. Jourdan, myself, and probably to Dr. Owsley, for a close of the discussion. But Mr. Jourdan was still unwilling, till he had consulted his friends, how the thing was going among the people in general. They told him that it had gone in his favor, and that he need not keep back on that account any longer. He told them, Mr. Stamper was out, for he had said very little more to the purpose than he had said the day before, and that he was confident, should the debate last one day longer, he could say nothing to the point. However, under the impression that it had gone in his favor, he yielded to Mr. Linsey's eager request; though not more than half through his arguments. They then went into the discussion, which was to end that evening. It proceeded much as formerly; Mr. Stamper still refusing to respond, and in this acted as Mr. M'Calla did when debating with Mr. Campbell.

It is believed by many, that Mr. Stamper's last speech was by far the weakest that he had made; being a repetition of what he had formerly said, with the exception of two or three quotations. In Mr. Jourdan's last discourse, he produced many positive declarations from sacred writ, to prove the soul cheering fact, that Jesus Christ is truly the Son of the living God. And with all the confidence of Divine Truth, and in full assurance that he had gained the point in debate; he gave the following challenge to the Methodist Clergy: Proposing to meet any one of them, who would engage to prove the *Trinity* a Bible doctrine - Or that the Methodist *Discipline* is authorized [sic] by the Great Head of the Church - Or that the *name* Methodist is not a schismatical name - Or should any be dissatisfied with the present discussion, and think he can do any better than Mr. Stamper has done, he is requested to make it known. And should any present feel disposed to accept this challenge, he will please to call upon him as soon as dismissed. But none of them opened their mouths to him upon the subject, and straight-way left the place.

Now, what I have stated, I think is correctly done; but lest I have erred, I will present this letter to the third Moderator, Dr. Owsley, for his inspection.

N. B. I am credibly informed that Mr. Jourdan made some proselytes, but that Mr. Stamper made none.

Elder Elihu H. Randolph, Moderator.[18]

Immediately following is the third moderator, Dr. Joel Owsley's, verifications of the accuracy of the account.

I have, with much care, read the foregoing detail, given by Mr. Randolph, concerning the debate between Mssrs. Stamper and Jourdan, held in Cumberland county, Ky, on the 8th, 9th and 10th days of April, 1829, and am of the opinion, that the statements contained are substantially true, so far, however, as I myself were in the possession of the facts. I attended the debate throughout, and was

---

[18] *Christian Messenger*, (April 1830), Vol. 4, No. 5, pp. 116-119.

very much delighted with the spirit there manifested, and the good order and harmony that prevailed with both parties. I was also in possession of some of the preliminaries of the debate, as settled on by the parties, and they are also properly detailed, so far as I can at this time recollect.

Joel Owsley, *Moderator.*
Burkesville, March 10th, 1830.[19]

Following that, is an explanation by the editor of the *Christian Messenger*, Barton W. Stone, as to his reason for publishing the letters.

Such publications as the above is [sic] a little foreign from the design of the Messenger, yet it was believed necessary at this time in order to rescue the truth and its advocate, brother Jourdan, from disgrace. We pretend not to say with whom the report originated, nor are we concerned. We hope this will be sufficient to correct it. We wish no farther [sic] details of the subject, nor shall we further notice them.

Editor.[20]

Thus we see the conflicts that John Mulkey and his associates faced in their labors.

Such were the pleas from these pioneer preachers that sought for the *Ancient Order of Things.*

They stood on a firm foundation, as they took their authority from only one source - the Bible.

They enjoined nothing upon men which God had not already required through His revelation.

But they would not allow their plea to be yoked to the whims, opinions, doctrines, or dictates of men; for upon such foundations, these preachers of old had already seen the religious world divided.

---

[19] *Christian Messenger*, (April 1830), Vol. 4, No. 5, p. 119.
[20] *Ibid*, p. 119.

A History of the Mill Creek ("Old Mulkey") Church
Tompkinsville, Kentucky

Chapter 8

The Passing of an Era

The death of John and Philip Mulkey marked the end of what one might call the pioneer days of the *Restoration Movement* in Southern Kentucky, Northern Tennessee, and Southern Illinois; where Philip had moved and established other New Testament churches.

Those who knew them and were acquainted with their labors for the *Ancient Order of Things* knew them to be dedicated men who had given their lives in service to spreading the simple Gospel of Christ.

As we have already pointed out, neither John, Philip, nor Isaac were active writers, thus their influence was more or less confined to their preaching efforts.

As generations passed the work of the Mulkeys became buried in obscure documents; very few with either John's, Philip's, or Isaac's signature attached to them.

E. Clayton Gooden has well noted:

> ...Disciples of Christ historians have given little credit to John Mulkey, usually dismissing his work in a sentence or two. Yet, this

outstanding pioneer preacher was one of the first voices heard on behalf of the restoration movement [1]

The credit that Gooden applies to John Mulkey is well deserved. Truly, Mulkey was one at the forefront of the plea for a return to New Testament Christianity. It is indeed a shame that he has been given so little credit for the groundwork that he prepared in Southern Kentucky and Northern Tennessee.
But the strength in numbers of the Church of Christ in this region of the world is a living testimony to the unselfish labors of this man and those associated with him.

Of those men that have stood out in historical books concerning this period, those who wrote the most appear to be those that are mentioned the most; and for good reason - for more was preserved through their pens.

One such was Alexander Campbell. Anyone who is at all acquainted with a history of the *Restoration Movement* is well aware of the influence of Campbell. But again, most of the credit that Campbell received was due to the great amount of written material that he left behind.
To indicate just how active Campbell's pen was during the formative years of the reformation, his biographer, Robert Richardson, noted:

> ...during the first seven years, ending July 4th, 1830, he [Alexander Campbell] issued of his own works, from his little country printing-office, no less than forty-six thousand volumes.[2]

Obviously, had John, Philip, or Isaac Mulkey been that engaged in writing, their ministry for the cause would of necessity have earned them much more attention.

But, let it be observed, that about the time that Alexander Campbell arrived on American soil to join his father Thomas Campbell (1809), John

---

[1] E. Clayton Gooden, January, 1965 issue of the *Discipliana*, reprinted in *The Kentucky Explorer*, February, 1993, p. 24.

[2] Robert Richardson, *Memoirs of Alexander Campbell*, Vol. 2, p. 51.

and Philip Mulkey were already making their stand for the *Ancient Order*, that being the division of the Mill Creek Baptist Church, the event taking place that same year November 18,1809.

While it is true that Campbell certainly reached more people through his writing efforts, it cannot be said that his ministry overshadowed that of the Mulkey's service in value, for much of the credit for the spread of the Gospel throughout the isolated wilderness territory of Southern Kentucky, Northern Tennessee, and Southern Illinois rests upon the Mulkeys.

John Mulkey departed this life on December 13, 1844 at 12:45 A.M. at the age of 71, just one month short of his 72nd birthday.

In penning Mulkey's obituary, Isaac T. Renau noted that in fifty-one years of preaching, John Mulkey had delivered ten thousand sermons.[3]

John's brothers Philip and Isaac are equally deserving of much more credit than they have been given by church historians, although less is known of them than their brother John.

In Philip's obituary in the *Millennial Harbinger* in January 1844, the following is noted about his service as a minister of the Gospel:

Little Muddy, Ill.
January 1844

"Elder Mulkey fell asleep in Jesus, at his residence in Franklin County, Illinois, on the evening of the 26th of the present month, in the 69th year of his age, having spent his life since early youth in the service of the Redeemer.

"Father Mulkey is supposed to have been the first who taught the ancient gospel in Tennessee. He was also the father of the restoration in the South of Illinois. Many Churches in both those states were planted by him, and many followers of Christ regard him as their spiritual father.

---

[3] Isaac T. Renau, "Obituary," *Christian Review*, Vol. II, No. 5 (May 1845), p.120. See also, Earl Irving West, *Search for the Ancient Order*, Vol. 1, p. 255.

"He suffered a long illness with patience, looking forward with joyous anticipation of that redemption which was drawing nigh. 'Blessed are the dead who die in the Lord, for they rest from their labors and their works follow them!'" [4]

In a history of Franklin County, Illinois, Philip Mulkey is given the following credit:

> Philip Mulkey settled the 7th settlement in Franklin County in 1814-1815, along with the Tinsleys and others around Tyrone, which is now Christopher and Mulkeytown, Illinois. The Mulkey family, after whom Mulkeytown was named, with their relative John Kirkpatrick, organized the first Christian Church in the state, in Tyrone Township in 1818.[5]

In his record of the history of the church at Mulkeytown, Illinois, Marion Silkwood noted the following:

> The Mulkeytown Christian Church was organized at the home of John Kirkpatrick in the year 1818 on what is now known as the Reid farm two and one-half miles northwest of Mulkeytown on Little Muddy C reek and was the first Christian Church organized in the state of Illinois. In 1823 they built a meeting house, (as they called it) on Four Mile Prairie five and one-half miles southeast of John Kirkpatrick's home, where they met each first day of the week to break bread and worship in the real gospel way .
> In the year 1835 Old Mulkeytown c a m e into existence a s a trading post and it took its name from the Mulkey family, Tinsley Mulkey being the first to establish a store there...
> For more than a century the Mulkey and Kirkpatrick families were identified with the church...

---

[4] *Millennial Harbinger*, (January 1844).
[5] *The Mulkeys of America*, (private printing, 1982), p. 417.

Philip Mulkey and wife came to Mulkeytown in their old age; he and his brother John had been in town many times before on preaching trips but had always returned to Tennessee...[6]

John Mulkey is buried in the Vernon Community (east of Tompkinsville, Kentucky, just off Highway 216) beside his wife Elizabeth on land that they once owned.

Philip Mulkey is buried in the Mulkeytown Cemetery alongside his wife Ruth.

The Mulkey Families

The preachers John, Philip, and Isaac Mulkey were three of nine children (4 boys and 5 girls) born to Jonathan and Nancy (Sarah) Mulkey. Apparently, Jonathan Mulkey Jr. was the only one of the four boys that didn't become a minister. The nine children include:

1. John Mulkey, born Jan. 14, 1773 at Fairforest, South Carolina, died 1844.

2. Philip Mulkey, born April 3, (or 6th), 1775 at Fairforest, South Carolina, died, 1844.

3. Mary Mulkey, born about 1777, died probably between 1866 and 1870, married, Thomas Means.

4. Nancy Mulkey, born March 9, 1780, married — Billingsley.

5. Sarah (Sally) Mulkey, born about 1781, married Bayliss, second marriage to — Marrs.

6. Jonathan Mulkey Jr., born 1784 or 1787.

7. and 8. Rebecca Mulkey and Isaac Mulkey, twins; born, May 17, 1788; Rebecca married William Slaughter Jr. and Isaac married Rachel Hampton; Isaac died 1855.

9. Elizabeth Mulkey, born about 1790, married John Murray.[7]

---

[6] *The Mulkeys of America*, (private printing, 1982), p. 417-418.
[7] *The Mulkeys of America*, p. 79.

John and Elizabeth (Betsy) Hays Mulkey raised 10 children, and four of their six sons became ministers. Jonathan, and possibly Sally, were born in Tennessee, the rest at Mill Creek near Tompkinsville, Kentucky. The 10 children include:

1. Jonathan Howard Mulkey 1795-1860, married, Talitha Hardin.
2. Sally Mulkey 1797, married, Jacob Johnson.
3. Mary (Polly) Mulkey 1799, married, Joel Wright Harlan.
4. Joseph Mulkey 1800.
5. Philip Mulkey 1802-1893, married, Martha H. Martin.
6. Isaac Mulkey 1804, married, Abigail Ragin.
7. John Newton Mulkey 1806, married Nancy Lough.
8. James Harlan Mulkey 1809, married, Sarah A. Martin.
9. Elizabeth (Betsy) Mulkey 1811. 10.
Nancy Mulkey 1814.[8]

Philip and Ruth Mulkey were married in 1795, but it is known that their first boy wasn't born until 1806. Following is a list of their 10 children in the probable order and dates of birth:

1. Sarah Mulkey (1796?), married John Stacy.
2. Alice Mulkey 1797-1872/1884?, married John Tinsley.
3. Rebecca Mulkey 1799, married William Tinsley.
4. Edith Mulkey 1804-1838, married John Kirkpatrick.
5. John Minton Mulkey 1806-1849, married Matilda Scantlin.
6. Ruth Mulkey 1807-1843, married Robert Kirkpatrick.
7. Matilda Mulkey 1808?, was blind from childhood.
8. Jonathan Howard Mulkey 1809-1867, married (Alice) Lucinda Scantlin.
9. Caleb Franklin Mulkey 1812-1876, married Lucretia Scantlin.
10. William Tinsley Mulkey 1815, married Elizabeth Kirkpatrick.[9]

---

[8] *The Mulkeys of America*, (private printing, 1982), p. 88.
[9] *Ibid*, p. 420.

A History of the Mill Creek ("Old Mulkey") Church
Tompkinsville, Kentucky

Chapter 9

The Next Generation

The spiritual influence of the Mulkey family upon Southern Kentucky and Northern Tennessee was carried on in the ministry of John and Elizabeth's fourth son (seventh child) John Newton Mulkey, who was born near Tompkinsville, Kentucky in 1806.

John Newton's grave is in the churchyard of the old Mill Creek Church, just a few steps north of the log meetinghouse where his father made the first stand in Southern Kentucky for the *Ancient Order of Things*, three years after John Newton's birth.

It is even claimed by some church historians that it was in this old meetinghouse that three generations of Mulkey preachers all preached from the same pulpit, all on the same day; John Newton, his father John, and his grandfather Jonathan.[1]

But John Newton's most memorable labors for the reformation would not be at the Mill Creek Church, but rather, first in remote Monroe County in a small community known as Martinsburg, between Kettle Creek and the Cumberland River, in the southeastern part of the county; then later in the city of Glasgow, Kentucky, in Barren County.

John Newton's Early Life

John Newton Mulkey was born February 11, 1806, two miles southeast of Tompkinsville, Kentucky, and was immersed into Christ in early life by Samuel Dewitt. He was married to Nancy Laugh in Kentucky, October 7, 1824, and began to preach in East Tennessee about the year 1831. His first sermon west of the Cumberland Mountains was a short discourse on *"The Weekly Meeting of the Church to Break Bread."* It was delivered in the

---

[1] W.C. Rogers, *Recollections of Men of Faith*, p. 224.

summer of 1832, in the Liberty meetinghouse, two miles west of the mouth of Wolf River, Clay County, Tennessee.[2]

John Newton Moves Back to Kentucky

John Newton Mulkey spent some time in the state of Tennessee. He later returned to his home state of Kentucky in 1833 or 1834, and again settled in Monroe County, but did not do much preaching for the first four or five years.[3] Later, circumstances urged him to take up the ministry at Martinsburg.

Following is John Rogers' account of how John Newton Mulkey came to be established in the ministry in Southern Kentucky.

> His [John Newton Mulkey] entering the ministry was rather peculiar, as might be said, from the force of circumstances. Returning from Tennessee, he found a few brethren within and around a small village called Martinsburg, situated on the Cumberland River, and at the mouth of a creek on which he had settled. These persons had given themselves to the Lord, through the labors of his father, and now it was proposed that they give themselves to one another, that they might keep house for the Lord. It was something new and strange to the people of that day, and of that section, to see professing Christians meet on the Lord's day and attempt to worship God without the aid of a preacher.
>
> There was much prejudice against this unheard-of procedure in the minds of honest people, and this must, if possible, be removed. No one could be found better able to do this, either publicly or privately, than John Newton Mulkey. He searched the Scriptures daily to know the teachings of Christ and his apostles on this special point, and then attempted to show his brethren and the people at large, who were inquiring for the truth, that the disciples met together on the first day of the week to break bread, and that this was the leading object before their minds in coming together, and not to hear preaching, as is

---

[2] *Recollections of Men of Faith*, p. 226.
[3] *Ibid*, p. 226.

generally supposed, although preaching on such an occasion is certainly scriptural and calculated to accomplish great good. He was greatly blessed in being a good singer, at least so regarded in that day. His voice was strong and full of melody, and he sang with the spirit and the understanding. When only sixteen years of age, one year after his conversion, I heard him sing a song beginning –

"There is a school on earth begun,
Supported by the Holy One;"

and although only a small boy, being eleven years of age, I well remember how I gazed into the bright, happy face of the singer, in the enjoyment of sins forgiven and the hope of heaven. I could not appreciate all then, but I trust the Lord will never allow me to forget that homely song, or the sweet cadences that then touched my young and tender heart.

O, what power there is in sacred song! Would that I could sing as I have heard my brother sing. But I trust I shall sing by and by, when I reach the better land, and join my brother in Christ the Lord.

Bro. Mulkey sang, read the Scriptures and prayed on the occasions of which we speak. In attending to the Lord's Supper, he was the only one for years among the brethren who was competent to officiate at the table. For some weeks he would do little more in presiding than sing, return thanks, partake with his brethren, adjourn, and go home to meet on the next Lord's day.

Not many meetings passed, however, until he began, unconsciously, to expound the Scriptures to the brethren, and urge upon them the necessity of Christian duty and privilege.

Being a good reader, and a fine singer, and very earnest in prayer, as well as clear and forcible in his comments on the lessons selected for each first day of the week, it was not long until his brethren and the people generally in the neighborhood regarded him as the one who promised to become successful in the ministry.

The brethren urged upon him to extend his comments, to enlarge his talks on the selected portions to be read, and although modest and diffident, he resolved if possible to comply with their request. Hence, during the week he would take the Bible and open to the lesson for the first day and read and ponder as best he could until the time came for him to lead and to speak. His loving heart was full, and he was so enabled to explain the Scriptures that soon those outside of the church would come in to see and to hear for themselves. His faith, growing day by day, so increased that he became strong, not in self, but in the Lord and in the power of his might. Thus in a short time he was prepared to deliver set discourses on chosen themes. His fame could not be confined, but went abroad. He was now invited to preach in schoolhouses and private dwellings. The pleasant shade of the trees in summer and fall was as good a house as he wanted. Calls came from all parts of Southern Kentucky - from friends of the truth - to pay them a visit, hold meetings, organize churches and build up the cause of the Master. Poor as he was, and working with his own hands to support his family, he never failed to respond when in his power to do so. He would often go a distance and hold a successful meeting and return home after an absence of two or three weeks and not bring money enough with which to buy his wife a calico dress. But like the majority of the pioneers of the Reformation, he loved to preach the gospel, for his soul was filled with the love of God, and he felt bound to do what he could to save the lost ones around him. He never thought much about the pay in money; all he cared for was to feed, and clothe, and educate his family, and then the great matter was to lay up treasures in heaven, by doing good.

The foregoing are some of the foot-prints of Bro. Mulkey in the path of life up to the years of 1827 and '28, but not all.

Bro. Mulkey never engaged in doing anything worth doing that he did not work at with all his might. That trait in his character he came by honestly, for his father was a man of much energy, and labored hard in all his undertakings, especially in preaching what he believed to be the truth.

The following incident will show how highly Bro. Mulkey was esteemed by his neighbors who differed from him religiously: Shortly after moving to Warren [Rogers probably meant Monroe or Barren County] county, Ky., he was invited to visit a locality entirely new to him, all persons being strangers except one man, a Cumberland

Presbyterian, who had once lived near him, and with whom he was well acquainted. He began preaching in a school-house, and soon some of the most respectable citizens, not belonging to any religious body, as well as many intelligent and enthusiastic Methodists; also not a few honest and fair-minded Cumberland Presbyterians became obedient to the faith. For miles around the interest spread among all classes, who crowded to hear the new preacher and the new gospel - at least new to them. But the excitement among the sects was not only intense, but very bitter. They were not able to answer the scriptural arguments they had heard, and consequently they resorted to abuse of character. They first whispered hard things about Bro. Mulkey, a certain Mr. "They Say" figuring very largely in all that was said and done. Finally they spoke out with great boldness against his character. Col. A., an elder in the Cumberland Presbyterian Church, and once his neighbor, could stand it no longer. It was now his time to talk, and rest assured he was heard from. He was none of your milk-and-cider men - what he did, he did boldly, and he was a man of standing and much influence. He forthwith went to his friends and brethren and said: "Gentlemen, you have just got to dry up that ugly talk about the character of Mr. Mulkey; you may say what you please about his doctrine, for I have my objections to it as well as you, but as for Mr. Mulkey, I've known the man long and well; I've tried him as a neighbor and as a friend in time of need. He's an honest, upright man - a Christian gentleman. You can talk about his doctrine, but you shall not lay your hand on his character!" That was enough; it stopped the mouths of the gain-sayers, for when Col. A spoke, they knew what he meant. It was not at all necessary for him to repeat the dose.

In the year 1843, Bro. Mulkey held a meeting with Elder Sandy E. Jones, in the town of Thompkinsville [Tompkinsville], within a few miles of where he was born, reared, and became a member of the church. Bro. Jones did most of the preaching, Bro. Mulkey the exhorting and the baptizing. This was a glorious meeting, resulting in 132 by confession and baptism. And this is only one of many meetings of large ingatherings [sic] that might be named, held by our dear and self-sacrificing brother in the Lord. [4]

Thus we see through the writings of W. C. Rogers that John Newton Mulkey was following in the footsteps of the *Restoration Movement* that had so aptly been established by his father before him.

And, like his father before him, John Newton was not only an able preacher, but he was also well respected by those in the community; even those that did not share his love for the old paths of New Testament Christianity.

But John Newton would face an even more severe test of his ability, as Rogers further explains concerning his labors to expel the influence of the Mormons.

John N. Mulkey Challenges the Mormons

Ironically, Mormonism had come to be an influence through one of the very preachers that had worked closely with Alexander Campbell, his father Thomas Campbell, and Walter Scott, years earlier; Sidney Rigdon.

In his memoirs of Alexander Campbell, Robert Richardson notes that Sidney Rigdon and his brother-in-law Adamsom Bentley, two Baptist preachers, visited Campbell in the summer of 1821. Bentley had been instrumental in helping form the Mahoning Baptist Association in what was called the Western Reserve territory of Ohio in 1820. At this meeting at Campbell's house in 1821, Alexander discussed his views of New Testament Christianity, and Rigdon, after listening throughout the night, noted the next morning "that if he had within the last year taught and promulgated from the pulpit one error, he had a thousand."[5]

In 1822, through Alexander Campbell's influence, and Rigdon's

being favorable to the reformation, Rigdon was induced to accept a call to preach for the church at Pittsburgh.[6]

---

[4] *Recollections of Men of Faith*, pp. 209-214.

[5] Robert Richardson, *Memoirs of Alexander Campbell*, Vol. 2, p. 45.

[6] *Ibid*, Vol. 2, p. 47.

When Campbell debated McCalla in Kentucky, late in 1823, Rigdon went along and took notes, and later assisted Mr. Campbell when the debate was being prepared for publication.[7]

Having been introduced to Walter Scott by Campbell, earlier, the two men grew so close that the respective congregations of both men united following the meeting of the Redstone Association in 1823.[8]

For the next few years Rigdon was closely associated with Scott and the Campbells and an active participant in the reformation. But Rigdon's good standing took a different turn in the late 1820's.

Richardson describes it like this:

> Toward the close of this year (1830) the delusion of Mormonism began its course in Northern Ohio. Chief amongst its promoters appeared Sydney [sic] Rigdon, who was believed, upon good evidence, to have been its originator...
>
> He (Rigdon) was ambitious of distinction, without the energy and industry necessary to secure it, and jealous of the reputation of others, without the ability to compete with them. Floating upon the tide of popular excitement, he was disposed to catch at anything which, without demanding labor, might serve for his advancement, and was naturally led to seek in deception the success which he found denied to indolence.
>
> It appears that, while living in Pittsburgh, he was connected with one of the printing-offices, and obtained access to the manuscript of a romance written by a former Presbyterian preacher - a Solomon Spaulding - who, adopting the style of the Bible history, had, for his amusement, given a fanciful account of the nations inhabiting Canaan before the time of Joshua, and described with great minuteness, their modes of life, wars, migrations, etc. He attributed also in it the settling of North America to the ten lost tribes, and, giving to his work the title of *"Lost Manuscript Found."* was wont to read portions of it frequently to his friends. Having copied or obtained possession of this

---

[7] Robert Richardson, *Memoirs of Alexander Campbell*, Vol. 2, pp. 71, 95.

[8] *Ibid*, Vol. 2, p. 99.

manuscript, Rigdon seems to have secretly occupied himself during several years in altering and arranging it to suit his purposes; and discovering, at Palmyra, New York, as early as 1827, a suitable coadjutor in the person of Joseph Smith, a pretended fortune-teller and discoverer of hidden treasure, noted for his idleness and love of everything marvelous and mysterious, he arranged with him the plan of future operations. Accordingly, in 1830, it was duly announced that Smith had by an express revelation disinterred certain golden plates, on which were inscribed, in the "reformed Egyptian character," important divine communications, giving an account of the ten lost tribes, the origin of the North American Indians and revelations designed to usher in "the latter days..."

...a book in manuscript was speedily produced, called the *"Book of Mormon..."*

Meanwhile, Rigdon had been for some time diligently engaged in endeavoring, by obscure hints and glowing millennial theories, to excite the imaginations of his hearers, and in seeking by fanciful interpretations of Scripture to prepare the minds of the churches of Northern Ohio for something extraordinary in the near future..." [9]

Thus Richardson credits the birth of Mormonism to Sidney Rigdon.

Soon after his ministry began at Martinsburg (Monroe County, Kentucky), John Newton Mulkey was called to face the Mormon influence which was attempting to spread its influence in the South.

W. C. Rogers gives the account as follows:

I remember an incident that greatly endeared him [John Newton Mulkey] to the religious denominations. It occurred in the early part of his ministry...

The Mormons, being routed from Independence, Mo., came to Hancock county Ill., and commenced building their great Temple in Nauvoo. They resolved to proselyte to the utmost of their ability, and they sent out their missionaries into all parts of the country (and they

---

[9] Robert Richardson, *Memoirs of Alexander Campbell*, Vol. 2, pp. 344-346.

didn't send fools - not by any means). Two of these came into the same country - but not into the immediate neighborhood - in which Bro. Mulkey lived. They began their cunning operations among the Methodists and Baptists, and a few scattering Cumberland Presbyterians. They got along finely until they walked out on their platform, claiming to have the power to work miracles, as did Christ and the apostles. Their plans were ingeniously made out and all their shrewd and plausible arguments were cut and dried, and an answer was easy prepared for every objection that could be offered to their positions. They read from the last chapter of Mark's Gospel, from Ephesians, 4th chapter, 1 Corinthians, 12th chapter, and so ingeniously argued that it seemed almost impossible to believe any other way than as they said. The sects, although unable to answer them or confound them, would not accept their doctrine. They called upon them to perform a miracle and then they would believe. The Mormons would readily excuse themselves by saying they were away from the body of faith - among unbelievers. This was not altogether satisfactory to the sects, notwithstanding they did not know just how to off-set it. It is said "the last straw breaks the camel's back," and the Mormons made a last argument that silenced the sects, and rendered them triumphant in the eyes of those belonging to no denomination. They said to the sects, "Do you not believe in an influence of the Holy Spirit, separate and apart, above and independent of the Word of God? Do you not believe that there is a mystery that cannot be explained by the finite mind, in this influence of the Holy Spirit? Now the reason you cannot work miracles is because you have no faith; if you had faith as a grain of mustard-seed, you could remove mountains - in truth you could do all things." Here the sects bowed their heads in silence; they could go no further - they were stranded - they gave up in despair. However, there was still left a glimmer of hope. Some one [sic] had heard of a preacher in the country by the name of Mulkey, who was well posted in regard to the doctrine of Mormonism, was a good speaker, and withal bold enough to attack the lion in his den. Send for him; possibly he can rid us of these pestilent fellows and give us a little rest. So a messenger was immediately dispatched for Bro.

Mulkey. He gave up his work at home, and went to the scene of action. He arrived at dusk - just in time to walk into the place of speaking as one of the missionaries began his discourse. He listened attentively and with great patience. His plans were all well prepared, and he knew as well as anyone exactly how to assail the enemy. The speaker had claimed the power to work miracles, had urged these claims vehemently, and defied the world to show to the contrary. At the conclusion of the services, Bro. Mulkey rose up and calmly asked for a confirmation of the claims set forth. The same old plea was set up - "among unbelievers - away from the body of faith." "No, sir," said Bro. Mulkey, "that will not answer; your plea is not good or sufficient; the ambassadors of Christ were able to do and did do just what was promised. Either work a miracle, or never again claim to be able to do so." The Mormons argued that the Savior on a certain occasion could not perform many mighty miracles because of unbelief. Bro. Mulkey replied that that was not to the point; that had the Savior performed no miracles at all it would not excuse them. "God at sundry times and in divers manners spake in time past unto the fathers by the prophets," and be it understood he confirmed all his communications. Your claim that God is now speaking from on high, through Joe (Joseph] Smith, to this generation. Now, I demand that you confirm what you say. You profess to be his ambassadors. The Mormons replied, "You would not believe should we do so." Bro. Mulkey said with emphasis, 'That's not the point under discussion, whether we would believe or not. You are here offering a new revelation to the people. As Joe Smith's ambassadors, confirm your message by the manifestation of miraculous power, or abandon your claim. I withstand you; you shall not turn this people away from their faith. If you are competent ambassadors, bring the hand of the Lord upon me, as Paul did upon Elymas the sorcerer, who withstood him while he was endeavoring to convert the deputy. Strike me blind if you can, or acknowledge that you are deceivers - impostors!"

This was too much for them; they could say no more - they were silent. Bro. Mulkey now turned upon them with more severity than ever, and remarked: "Gentlemen, we have no other words for you;

besides, we have no further use for you in this part of the country; the sooner you leave, the better. One word, now in closing, to my fellow-countrymen."

He then proceeded to show up Joe Smith and the apostate, Sidney Rigdon. How they had combined to so mar the manuscript of Solomon Spaulding by additions, subtractions and alterations that it could not be recognized. These men had agreed to offer to the world the most outlandish and corrupt delusion, or religion, or whatever you may please to call it, known in this, the nineteenth century. This was one of the grandest efforts of Bro Mulkey's life - at least so considered by all who heard him. Had he called for it, these professing Mormon ambassadors could easily have been placed on rails, and with tar and feathers adorned, allowed to ride out of the country. As it was, they saw proper to leave the next morning at dawn of day. The people were at rest, and John Newton Mulkey was ever afterward considered, not only the grandest man, but one of the best in that section of the country.[10]

Conflicts with the Mormons were not uncommon at that time, as a letter, reprinted from the *Christian Watchman*, in the *Christian Messenger*, reveals.

In that correspondence, October 12, 1832, a Mr. B. Pixley of Independence, Jackson County, Missouri, made the followed comments:

> ...They [Mormons] declare there can be no true church where the gift of miracles, of tongues, of healing, &c. are not exhibited and continued. Several of them, however, have died, yet none of them have been raised from the dead. And the sick, unhappily, seem not to have faith to be healed of their diseases. One woman, I am told, declared in her sickness, with much confidence, that she should not die, but here live and reign with Christ a thousand years; but unfortunately she died, like other people, three days after. They tell

---

[10] *Recollections of Men of Faith*, pp. 214-218.

indeed of working miracles, healing the sick, &c. &c. These things, however, are not seen to be done, but only said to be done...

Their first, best, great and celebrated preacher, Elder Rigdon, tells us the Epistles are not and were not given for our instruction, but for the instruction of a people of another age and country, far removed from ours, of different habits and manners; and needing different teaching: and that it is altogether inconsistent for us to take the Epistles written for that people at that age of the world, as containing suitable instruction for the people at this age of the world. The Gospels too, we are given by them to understand, are so mutilated and altered, as to convey little of the instruction which they should convey. Hence we are told a new revelation is to be sought, is to be expected, indeed is coming forthwith. Our present Bible is to be so altered and restored to its primitive purity, by Smith, the present prophet of the Lord, and some books to be added of great importance, which have been lost.

They profess to hold frequent converse with angels; some go, if we may believe what they say, as far as the third heaven, and converse with the Lord Jesus face to face. They baptize, saying, "I, John, the Messenger, baptize thee," &c.

More secretly, they are said to impart to their converts the gift of the Holy Ghost. They profess to know where the ark of the covenant, Aaron's rod, the pot of Manna,&c. &c. now remain hid...[11]

It is therefore seen that turning the tide on the influence of Mormonism in Southern Kentucky was no small task for John Newton Mulkey.

John Newton's Latter Years

According to W. C. Rogers, John Newton Mulkey dedicated himself to preaching New Testament Christianity, from the time he began laboring with the church at Martinsburg in Monroe County Kentucky (about 1839), until his death in Glasgow, Kentucky on September 26,1882.[12]

---

[11] Barton W. Stone, *Christian Messenger*, (February 1833), Vol. 7, No. 2, pp. 40-43.
[12] *Recollections of Men of Faith*, p. 226.

Rogers reveals a letter written by Isaac T. Reneau that tells of John Newton Mulkey's latter preaching career as follows:

> In the year 1850, some of the churches of Kentucky south of Green River sent delegates to Glasgow to for a "co-operation" of churches, in order to "call and send" a suitable evangelist to preach the gospel within their bounds. After organizing, the next business was to inquire, "Whom shall we send and who will go for us?" And as all eyes were fixed on Bro. Mulkey, and all said, "Newton Mulkey is the man," he was unanimously "called and sent." And in obedience to the will of the co-operation, as he expressed annually, he continued to preach five or six years with general success and profit.
>
> This eminent servant of the churches must have delivered, in the fifty-three years of his entire ministry, nearly *ten thousand* discourses, and immersed as many believers, at one meeting in Celina, Clay county, Tenn., in the summer of 1855, he immersed *one hundred and five persons in five days*. After having resigned his work to the Warren County Co-operation, and also to the Kentucky Missionary Board, Bro. Mulkey emigrated to Perry county, Ill., and after the death of his beloved wife returned to Kentucky and settled in Glasgow, making that his home for some eighteen months. He then married Nancy Evans, a Christian lady of that city.[13]

John Newton Mulkey's work with the church in Glasgow was conducted where Alexander Campbell had once preached, as is revealed by Barren County historian Cecil Goode:

> The noted Alexander Campbell visited Glasgow in 1823 and preached in the brick ell of Mrs. John H. Gorin's house. He came again in 1831; and as a result, it is reported that the Glasgow Baptist Church lost over half of it members to the new movement including its pastor, Joseph W. Davis, who led the defecting group...

---

[13] *Recollections of Men of Faith*, p. 227.

The first Christian Church [Glasgow] was organized in 1830...The church erected its first meeting house, on South Green Street.

Dr. R. H. Grinstead wrote about the Christian Church in a 1900 article in the *Glasgow Times*. The church was located on the corner of Green and Wayne Streets. It was a one story building built of various size logs, both knotty and smooth. A door swung on creaky wooden hinges. A window faced a pond that extended from Wayne Street to the Odd Fellows Building. It served as both a meeting house and school.

The benches were made of the very softest white logs that could be found and furnished by the contractor. They were split with the soft side up so that the adults and children could sit on them in as much comfort as possible.

Sunday was recognized as a day to break bread, with preaching a secondary consideration. Every member of the following families was present - the Trabues, James, Eubanks, Billy Grinstead, Preston Ritter, and others. Watts Hymn Books were used, and there was the soul-stirring preaching of Stone, Creath, Campbell, Stelle and Mulkey.

Elder W. L. Porter wrote of the second building, probably inspired by Alexander Campbell. The site adjoined the log church on South Green Street, and was completed in 1837 on a lot donated by James Eubank and his wife. It was 60 x 40 feet on a site that rose 15 feet above the street level. There was a front platform, 15 feet wide, with steps extending the width of the church as an approach. There were two front doors, the right one for the men and the left one for the women, who seated themselves on their respective sides.[14]

In that same work, it is also noted that,

---

[14] Cecil Goode, Woodford L. Gardner, Jr., *Barren County Heritage*, "Churches", p. 174.

John Newton Mulkey was a well-known Christian Church minister, who spent his last years in Glasgow, living on South Green Street near the present site of the South Green Street Church of Christ.[15]

Records also reveal that John Newton Mulkey preached at the Tompkinsville Church of Christ in 1854 and in 1856.[16]

John Newton Mulkey's Death

John Newton Mulkey died on Tuesday, at 7:25 p.m., September 26, 1882, at age 76 years, seven months, and 15 days.[17]

Following John Newton Mulkey's death, Isaac T. Reneau had these remarks for the family:

> That the bereaved family may long remember his noble person, his valuable instruction and his pious example, is the prayer of *their* brother in Christ, and *his* true yoke-fellow in the gospel of Christ for forty-four years.
>
> Isaac T. Reneau [18]

The following letter was received from John Newton Mulkey's daughter in Illinois, and read to him while he was dying, but still conscience and able to understand:

> Dear Father: - It is with a sad heart I write these lines to you at this time. I could write to others of the family all I would write to you, but as I am deprived of sitting by you and talking with you of the sufferings and conflicts of this life, and of the bright hope beyond, I wish to write to you.
>
> I have many things I would like to say to you. The first and most important of all is, that I thank you from the bottom of my heart for

---

[15] Cecil Goode, Woodford L. Gardner, Jr., *Barren County Heritage*, "Churches", p. 173.

[16] Tompkinsville Church of Christ, *Congregational History*, Bulletin printed, November 16, 1986.

[17] *Recollections of Men of Faith*, p. 227.

[18] *Ibid* , p. 227.

the manner in which I was brought up; for the Christian influence which you exerted over me in my earliest days, and for your encouraging me to fidelity. How often have I thanked God that I was blessed with such a father and mother! Who could tell what I might have been had I not been so blessed? It encourages me to exert a Christian influence over my own children. They may see the folly of their way and turn to God, who will abundantly pardon. You cannot know how much I wish to be with you, and especially now, that I might help wait on you, and in some measure return the kindness which you have so often bestowed on me. But alas! many miles stretch between my willing hands and your suffering frame. I know you will be well cared for; you have those around you that will not forsake you, that cannot forget you; and therefore I will try to submit to my lot in this distress and in all others. We have much in this life that is hard to bear, but it is short - it will soon be over - and then, if faithful, we shall enter into that blissful eternity where the weary are at rest.

Do not suffer uneasiness about me, dear papa, for I am fixed in my purpose. I will not let anything prevent my devotion. I will, by the grace of God, stand firm as a rock to the last. I will "run with patience the race that is set before us, looking to Jesus, the author and finisher of the faith." I cannot preach, but I can talk to those around me, and encourage them to fidelity, and in my humble way I will do all I can to bring souls to Christ.

Now, dear papa, I shall have to say farewell! and if it is for the last time in this life, I feel sure that we shall meet again, and as the poet says –

> "Just so our pleasant friendship leaves
> A fragrant memory;
> And among life's garnered sheaves
> For long eternity,
> May not we at last discover,
> Tis for us a joy forever?'"
> Your loving daughter, LYDIA LISENBY.[19]

---

[19] *Recollections of Men of Faith*, p. 228-229.

A History of the Mill Creek ("Old Mulkey") Church
Tompkinsville, Kentucky

Appendix-A

John Mulkey, "A Circular Letter Addressed to the Christian Churches in the Western Country"
[printed by] J.A. Woodson, Glasgow, Ky. 1821

[1] Dear Brethren:

I have lately seen the Minutes of the Stockton Valley Association of Baptists, for the year 1820 - and in these minutes I find myself charged with denying that I ever have been excommunicated from the Baptist Union. But they assert that I have been regularly dealt with, and excommunicated for heresy and contempt for the church. Consequently, I stand implicated with the charge of telling that which is not true. And in as much as the honor and success of the Gospel greatly depends on the credit of religious professors, and especially the good standing of Gospel Ministers, I feel myself duty bound, in order that I may do justice to my own personal character, and also to the cause which I have espoused, to give you and the rest of my fellow

---

[1] E. Clayton Gooden, *A Fork in the Road*, Original 1821 letter reprinted in its entirety, pp. 199-211, (Copy in Christian Theological Seminary Library, Indianapolis, IN).

citizens a correct statement of facts, relative to my separation from the Baptist Church, and then, leave everybody to judge how far the implication or charge against me is just.

Then I will observe, that it is generally well known, that some years ago a dissatisfaction took the doctrine of unconditional Election, and some other subjects; which led to much disputation, and finally terminated in an entire separation of myself and a number of others from the Baptist Church. The particulars of which separation I shall now proceed to state, with the candor of one who is sensible that the eye of God is upon him, and with as much correctness as my knowledge and recollection of the facts will enable me.

At the August meeting in the year 1809, myself and my opponents finding that we could not settle our differences, among ourselves, agreed to call on five of the neighboring churches, to aid us. The following October was the time agreed upon. They accordingly attended, by their delegates, took their seats and acted in conjunction with the church. The brethren, who considered me in error, then proceeded to exhibit charges against me - respecting my doctrinal views - my manner of preaching, etc. And indeed the way that some of them seemed to view my doctrines, it looked like I had gone far from the truth. However, I attended to each charge distinctly, and honestly pointed out my own views of those doctrines; and then proceeded to defend myself and my doctrines, as well as I at that time was able. And when I had gone through, and every subject was sufficiently investigated, the question was then put by the acting moderator (Elder Robert Stockton), *"For all who justify brother John Mulkey, to hold up their right hand,"* - and the majority was large in my favor. Consequently no more could be done against me at that time. And the helps that visited us returned, and left our affairs unsettled.

On the second Saturday in November we met again; and after meeting was opened, I proposed to the brethren, that we drop our disputes, and try to bear with each other, and live in peace, and perhaps we might, in time, come to a better understanding. But this proposal was utterly refused - and it was replied *"never till you come back to the ground you started from."* Thinking the impossible, agreeable to my present views; and being wearied with contention, I made another proposal, as the last alternative. And that was, if we could not live together in peace, that we agree to part in peace and each party do as well as they could. To this proposition I do not recollect one dissenting voice. And so the division immediately took place, and my opponents so far ratified the motion for the division, that they then called on all who were determined to stand to their old constitution, to come forward and have their names enrolled. I also called on all who felt like withdrawing from all human rules and man-made laws, to remove and give place to our brethren, to proceed in their own way. We accordingly did so; and I verily consider we were thus separated by mutual consent of parties; and from that day I have never considered myself a member of the Baptist Church - having dissented and left them on account of these rules and their manner of trying to enforce them; which to me appeared calculated to prevent free enquiry and to lord it over my faith.

Thus I was compelled to dissent or hypocritically conceal my real views of the Gospel. I can honestly say, I did love the brethren, and I do not feel like I should have left them, if I could have lived with them in peace, and the enjoyment of my religious liberty, at the same time. We who had withdrawn agreed to meet on the next Saturday. We met accordingly, and after solemn prayer to Almighty God for his direction and presence, we proceeded to enquire what plan we were to pursue.

After much deliberation and free conversation on every subject that came under our view, we finally concluded that all human creeds and confessions of faith were the works of fallible man and consequently they were imperfect and contradictory to each other and also that they had been the cause of many, if not most of the divisions in the church of God; likewise that they all had their zealous advocates, and, of course were calculated to divide Christians, and keep them apart. And further, believing that Christ is the great head of the church and King of Zion, the only Christian lawgiver, and that he had given a sufficiency of laws, rules and regulations, for the government of his church and people. We proceeded to unite ourselves as a Christian Society, agreeable to our best views of the Gospel; having, as we hoped first given to our Lord - we then gave ourselves to each other, by the will of God, to be subject to Christ and to each other in the Gospel, taking the Holy Scriptures as the only rule of our faith and practice, we therefore receive all whom we believe Christ has received, with the exception only of such as have been excluded from other societies, for immoral conduct; in that case we esteem it our duty, first to confess their faith to their brethren whom they offended: but if any are cast off using this religious liberty, we freely receive them, - believing that Christ has made them free, and that liberty of conscience is a right that God has conferred on his intelligent creatures and none has the right to take it from them, seeing that they are to account to God alone, for their religious conduct. Thus we have lived together in peace and brotherly love, generally speaking, and have in no instance found any deficiency in the sacred rule we have adopted, but have reason to thank God and take courage.

But to return to the subject of the division -1 now appeal to both the churches and the numerous crowd of spectators who attended my trial, for the correctness of my statements. Was I not justified by the majority when the helps were acting with the church? I appeal to the Baptist brethren themselves, as well as others acquainted with the circumstances, if we did not separate at the next meeting, in the manner I have stated. I also appeal to the Baptists themselves to say if any act of excommunication had ever been passed against me before the above stated transactions. There circumstances were generally well known, for these things were not done in a corner. I had some thoughts of publishing these facts, with some reflections on the subject, eight or ten years ago, when the association published me in their minutes the first and second time, but declined it purely for the sake of peace, thinking surely they would be done with me now, and would leave us in peace.

But Behold! In 1820 I am again raised up to the view of the public, in black colors and perhaps 200 copies added above the former number of their minutes. And even now I should have remained silent on the subject, had I not been implicated in the manner I have in these minutes. For I can truly say that I have no desire to retaliate nor to expose these unseemly disputes to public view; knowing how inimical these things are to the progress of vital religion, knowing also, who hath said vengeance is mine, I will recompense saith the Lord. Looking at the various divisions, contentions and bitter envyings among professors of the holy religion of the meek and peaceful Savior, I often transfer to myself the feeling of King David, when he said, "O tell it not in Gath, publish it not in the streets of Askelon, lest the daughters of the uncircumcised triumph. But now I proceed to notice the statements made in the minutes of 1820, in which, I am charged with denying my having been excluded from the Baptist Union I reply that the ground on which I have and still do deny that in my judgment there is any legality or validity in said exclusion, will clearly appear from the foregoing statement of facts. But they proceed to say I have been regularly dealt with and excluded from the church at Mill Creek, for heresy, and contempt of the church for proof of which they refer to the records of the said church - and their minutes 1810 and 1812. Now, notwithstanding the whole of this testimony has been recorded by my opponents, yet I will attend to every part that relates to my supposed exclusion, as distinctly as I can. When I first applied for a perusal of the church record, I was not admitted to see it, but have since seen and taken a copy, which I will here transcribe, and let you judge of the propriety of the Association referring to them.

THE RECORD OF THE MILL CREEK CHURCH

October, 2nd Saturday, 1809 - church met agreeable to appointment, with helps, and proceeded to hear the charges exhibited against Brother John and other charges of a like nature, and when again hearing the charges exhibited and debated - we then concluded that he denied the essential doctrine of the Gospel; such as denying in our esteem, that Jesus Christ satisfied the demands of law and justice for his people or died as our surety, or that any man is saved by the righteousness of Jesus Christ, imputed to them also finally, for treating the church with contempt, and going away and leaving us in our unpleasant situation.[2]

This record made March meeting 1810 - Now let me ask what there is in all this, that will approve the assertion in the minutes of the Association, that I was regularly dealt with and excluded? Let a stranger read it and what sense can he make of it. He will find no name but brother John! He will find a record that seems to commence in October and close the next March! The truth is the above is only a record of the proceedings of the October meeting as far as the debated word - the rest we then concluded etc., being a conclusion they came to in the March following. This was done by the minority, months after the separation. And how does this affect me? They conclude that I denied the essential doctrines of the Gospel, and that, in their esteem, I denied Christ's death as satisfying law and justice, suretyship, imputed righteousness, etc. The reserve and caution made use of here, is very remarkable. We concluded, and in our esteem - why all this caution in stating their conclusion? I answer, for this plain reason, they charged me to this amount at my trial, and I publicly defend myself, by giving my views clearly and distinctly as I was able, pointing out at the same time, the Scriptural account of the atonement, as well as I could at that time. Therefore it stood them in hand to go out farther than to say, in our esteem, etc. And were it not for swelling this beyond any reasonable bounds

---

[2] *Minutes of the Mill Creek Baptist Church* No. 2, (October, 2nd Saturday 1809) p. 1.

for circular, I would here publish my views of those doctrines they charge me with denying, but as I can not [sic] do it now, my enemies must make their conclusions as they please, while

I shall attend to the subject in hand. Now it is [sic] not astonishing to see so respectable a body of men as Stockton's Valley Association of Baptists making such assertion, and referring to such testimony in which my name is not inserted at full length, none but my given name and not one word about exclusion, (— Though I do not receive every idea which some attach to the death of Christ, yet it is well known that I uniformly preach Christ and him crucified as the only way of life and salvation, and all the ground of our hope. — this is an explanatory note), or excommunication in it, nor any other act, only what they concluded about my doctrine and treating the church with contempt, and going away and leaving them, in their unpleasant situation. These it seems were their conclusions. But they do not state a thing that they did in consequence of these conclusions. In truth it is the most vague record I recollect ever to have seen. I always thought it incorrect and desired to have it corrected. Now if they had simply stated the proceedings of the October meeting of the churches and helps as they really occurred etc. that after the charges were stated and debated, the matter was put to a vote, and Brother John Mulkey was justified or acquitted by a large majority and the helps went home and left us with our difficulties unsettled. How much honor they would have done themselves and their cause, and the way would have been beautifully opened for the record of the next monthly meeting, which is as follows -

November 2nd Saturday, 1809 - church met and a division took place in the church, and those whose names are above written, declared that they would no longer continue under the constitution of this church and withdrew from us, consequently are no more of us.[3]

---

[3] *Minutes of the Mill Creek Baptist Church* No. 2, (November, 2nd Saturday 1809) p. 1.

I will here remark that though the record is a little vague, yet it states facts. The church met and a division took place. Now this is very correct, as far as it goes; and to this record I refer you for proof of some of the statements I have made on this division. But it then goes on, those whose names are above written, and no one name above written; of course this part of the record is entirely vague; but for this I will make an apology for them, some of the brethren told me, that when this record was made they designed recording all our names above but for the difficulty of getting all the names collected, they never did it. But with this exception the record is correct: first stating the division and secondly that as we had separated ourselves, and had withdrawn from their constitution, we consequently were no more of them. Certainly everyone knew that this was the consequence and by the very same consequence they were no more of us. But there is still not a word about my being regularly dealt with and excluded. Now how is the truth of that statement in the minutes to be supported, seeing the material witness has entirely failed to support it? The minutes of 1810 mention the Church at Mill Creek asking advice respecting John Mulkey's credentials, he having formally been a member and minister of said church, but now excluded from it. The church is advised to send two members of her body to request him to give them up; and if he does not, the church to exercise her own power at discretion.

The minutes of 1812 state that the Mill Creek Church demanded of John Mulkey his credentials as a minister and he refused to give them up. We therefore declare all his authority as a minister, received from our union, to be void, and we will be no longer accountable therefor [sic].

The minutes of 1820 declare that I have been regularly dealt with and excluded. Now I shall go on to compare all these statements together. In 1810 they first publish that I was excluded at the same time we find them advising the Church at Mill Creek how to act respecting credentials.

Now I ask, if the proceedings against me had been regular, why had not my credentials been demanded before that time? I answer, they had never been able to establish a censure on me until after I had left them: and my credentials had never been asked for, till it was done pursuant to the advice of the Association. And to my refusing to give them up, I will only remark that after they had made known, the church's request, I attended a church meeting of theirs, and told the church that I was willing to give them up on conditions, and if they would please hear I would state the conditions, but they refused to hear my statement, so there it dropt [sic]. But I will here state the conditions, on which I was willing to give them up, which was, that they rectify the church records, for I was apprehensive that the whole proceeding did not stand fair on their church book - and by this time I judge some of them think with me, that there should have been a more full and correct statement. For my own part I was always of opinion that it would be for the credit of religion, for the facts to be so stated, as to give correct and satisfactory information to any person, who might read the church book: and if this had been the case, and association had only published the same, they might have published it annually while I lived without interrupting me; likewise, if this had been done, I should have had no objection at all to giving them my credentials, as they were now of no use to me for the following reasons: First, I had not received my authority to preach from man, but from the King of Zion, and the call of the church by ordination, was an acknowledgement that believed that the Head of the Church had appointed me and called me to that great work. Secondly - The Christian Church now believed the same in respect to my call and qualifications for the ministry, that the Baptist Church had formerly believed, and had received not only as a minister of their body, but as a legally authorized minister, "already set apart by ordination" believing it nothing better than solemn trifling to be reordaining [sic] those who have already been ordained and set apart to the great work, in the presence of God and man. I was not recognized as a minister in one church alone, but the elders and brethren, when met in conference, acknowledged me as a minister, and sent me on some missionary tours with letters of recommendation, to the churches at large, to receive me as a regular minister to administer ordinances, and set in order such things as might be wanting among them. I have still some of those letters in my posession [sic], which testify my standing to be on fair ground, my ministry valid and good, so that I stood on at least as good basis as any other dissenter or nonconformist whatever. There has no act of exclusion ever taken place against me; but what equal acts and of equal force have been exhibited at some period or other, against all denominations of dissenters and nonconformists.

I suppose that some of the dear suffering brethren of the Baptist name, are yet alive in America, whose active zeal for the glory of God and the good of souls led them on in the way they esteemed to be right, without regard to the established order of the day, and they prospered in the good work of the Lord, though some of them suffered in prisons - and the cry against them was heretics, deceivers, etc. Their opposers could afflict them because they then had the legal power on their side. O that we could be duly thankful for the enjoyment of civil and religious liberty! That we are not bound by law to believe any of the absurd creeds of men, or to receive or practice anything in a religious way that our conscience does not approve, as consistent with the Word of God. A few words more and I am done with the subjects of the statements in the minutes of the Association, they refer to the records of the Mill Creek Church to prove that I have been regularly dealt with and excommunicated: we find that those records state no such thing, and fortunate for them, they do not, for if they had, you see from the nature of our division it would not have been true. We find it declared in the minutes of 1810, that I have been excluded, but you will see from the foregoing statements and from the records of the church, that they had no well-grounded authority for making such a statement, and therefore their testimony is not to be regarded; of course the minutes of 1820 stand on the same ground, so there I leave them, and freely submit the whole to the judgment of every candid reader.

And now dear brethren, having gone through the subject, I shall take the liberty of offering to you a few things for consideration, by way of advice and caution - for this is certainly a time to try men's souls. Our adversary, the Devil is going about like a roaring lion, seeking whom he may devour, and among the means of destruction devised by this arch enemy, the art of dividing Christians is none the least; if he can get us separated, and puffed up one against another, and to biting and devouring one another, he then has his ends in a fair way of being accomplished, knowing that a kingdom divided against itself can not [sic] stand. We ought therefore to defeat the purpose of Satan, by uniting as much as possible with all true Christians, without regard to name or party. We should strive to possess that enlargement of soul, that would enable us to pierce through the guise of human distinctions, and trace religious excellence among all orders of men. We need not expect to find the good or the bad exclusively in any one society. I find some humble, liberal souls of every name I am acquainted with; and such are unspeakably near to my heart and affections - let them bear what name they may, they are not filled with the spirit of self conceit or infallibility, setting up themselves and their party and condemning all who differ from them in name or opinion. Wherever such travel or reside they are doing and are uniting the people of God closer together, instead of separating them - their charity manifests itself, not only in their doctrines, but in their lives and conduct, in the world and among their fellow men. Such brethren you should receive, whenever they come to you, in the name of the Lord; for Christ says to such, he that receiveth you receiveth me, and he that heareth me receiveth Him that sent me; and he that despiseth you despiseth me. Now, if we, under the influence of a party spirit, or party feelings should reject or refuse to receive any that Jesus has sent to us, with his word of truth, it would be awful indeed, for in so doing we should reject the Savior also, without whom, we must be forever miserable.

Let us then be extremely careful to slight none, who have the spirit of Christ, and in receiving them we shall receive him. But on the other hand we must not be forgetful that the Great Shepherd laid down his life for his sheep, told us to beware of false prophets, who come to you in sheep's clothing, but inwardly they are ravening wolves. He says that by their fruits you shall know them. Now we are left at no loss to know what we are to understand by good fruit in the Scripture. The prophet Isaiah tells us the work of righteousness is peace and the effect of righteousness is quietness and assurance forever. Christ say [sic] "herein is my Father glorified, that ye bear much fruit" and Paul says, "the fruit of the spirit is love, joy, peace, etc."

Now it would not be amiss to take a little notice of the Scriptural account of the false prophets of old, some of them healed slightly, saying peace, when there was no peace - some of them ruled the people with cruelty, pushing with side and shoulder, and so scattering the flock. And the Lord said he would judge them - Ezekiel 24:20 I will judge between the fat cattle and the lean cattle - verses 23-24 "I will set up one shepherd over them - and I the Lord will be their God, and my servant David a prince among them" - verse 29 "and I will raise up for them a plant of renown" etc. The influence of false prophets and false religion is pointed out in the 65th chapter of Isaiah and the 5th verse, which says, "Stand by thyself, come not near to me, for I am holier than thou, these are a smoke in my nose, a fire that burneth all day."

The Scribes and Pharisees, when the Lord was among them, trusted in themselves that they were righteous and despised others, and this was condemned by our Lord as bad fruit: and he lets us know that except our righteousness exceed theirs, we shall in no case enter into the Kingdom of Heaven. Now if any come to you contending with zeal about opinions, forms and words, calculated to raise contentions, debates and strife; which are unprofitable and vain, they divide the flock laboring to build a party;

they push themselves with side and with shoulder; they set the people contending with each other, and cause them to fall out by the way: they spare no pains to make a proselyte, and when they have made him he is twofold a child of Hell than themselves: for they have the art to diffuse their own spirit into their proselytes and set them at variance with all who differ with them in opinion. By these means and the like, they influence their converts to become unsociable and cause them to become worse citizens than they were before they professed any religion at all.

Now it is easy to see that these things can not [sic] be the fruits of the religion of the Prince of Peace. But there are still other evil fruits produced by corrupt trees, that of defaming, reproaching and slandering those of different denominations from themselves. Many of them are manifestly like some in Jeremiah's days. Report, say they, and we will report it. They are engaged to circulate every evil report they can get hold of. Some individuals pass through the land, and every time they pass they have some evil to speak of some body [sic]. These are bad fruits; and such poor, miserable wretches are objects of pity, and also of contempt. What a disgrace to religion are such despicable characters, but though we are not to receive such, yet it is our duty to pity and pray for them. Their eyes are blinded; they are under strong delusions having men's persons in admiration because of advantage; their eyes are shut against the truth.

And how can they believe truth, who receive honor one from another. Tine Apostle John says, "He that denyeth that Jesus is come in the flesh is antichrist". The same apostle also says in his second epistle verse 10 "If there come any unto you and bring not this doctrine, receive him not into your house, neither bid him God speed, for he that biddeth God speed is partaker of his evil deed." Let us examine what this doctrine is, that the apostle says that they must bring - verse 4 "we have received a commandment from the Father" Verse 5 "not a new commandment, but that which we had from the beginning, that we love one another". Verse 6 "This is love, that we walk after his commandments, this is the commandment that ye have heard from the beginning, ye should walk in it".

Now this is plainly the doctrine named in the 10th verse, that is love, this is the commandment we had from the beginning; if any bring not this doctrine, receive him not. You see its opposite in the 7th verse, deceivers who confess not that Jesus Christ has come in the flesh, this is a deceiver and an antichrist. Now if we do not love one another according to the commandment we had from the beginning, we transgress and abide not in the doctrine of Christ; and though we may profess to know him, yet in words we deny him, and of course shall be found under the characters of deceivers. The same apostle says in his first Epistle chapter one verse 7, "But if we walk in the light we have fellowship one with another, and the blood of Jesus Christ, his son, cleanseth from all unrighteousness". Second chapter verse 9, "He that saith he is in the light, and hateth his brother, is in darkness even until now." Verse 10 "He that loveth his brother, abideth in the light". Chapter 3 verse 14 "We know that we have passed from death unto life, because we love the brethren: he that loveth not his brother, abideth in death". Read the fourth chapter through, but let the 20th verse be solemn warning to every one, [sic] who is not governed by the principles of love. "If any man say, 'I love God' and hateth his brother, he is a liar". Jesus has told us, "By this shall all men know that ye are my Disciples, if ye love one another". This is the doctrine of Heaven, the marks of Christ's sheep and the fruits by which we know and distinguish them from others. In order that we may walk safely, we must walk close to our shepherd and follow him; for Jesus says "He that followeth me shall not walk in darkness, but shall have the light of life" again "If any man doeth his will, he shall know of the doctrine, whether it be of God". If we are duly engaged in doing his will, and following the Savior, we shall know the shepherd's voice, and shall not follow strangers; we shall delight in things that become sound doctrine, and love all men and pity and pray for worst enemies. Finally our light will shine and truth will prevail. Indeed, brethren, we have reason to rejoice that notwithstanding the floods of opposition and torrents of abuse that have poured forth from various quarters, yet truth is prevailing. Gospel light is shining. Error and sectarian bigotry is in many instances giving way; and the Kingdom of the Redeemer is spreading.

For these things we should be truly thankful, and willingly suffer for his name's sake; yea, and rejoice in our persecutions, which we bear for truth's sake. Our Lord foretold us these things, and directs us to rejoice and be exceeding glad for so persecuted they the prophets which were before you dear brethren; you know that these things have been the lot of the faithful in all ages. We ought to be patient under all these things, when our enemies charge us with denying the Savior, why need we mind that, seeing we know whom we have believed; yea we know him and the power of his resurrection, and the fellowship of his sufferings. When they charge us with denying his blood, we know its efficacy on our hearts, that it purifies and cleanses from all sin. And while our adversaries charge us with making Christ a part of our Savior, and denying the efficacy of his blood, some of them deny that Christ died in any special sense, for any but a part of the human race; and also deny that his blood cleanses from all sin while we are well assured that he has died in the most proper and unlimited sense, for the sins of the whole world, and we exult in the efficacy of that blood, which does cleanse the believer from all sin. But it makes but little difference what we are charged with, our trust is in God, and those who trust in man or maketh flesh their arm are accursed.

Dear Brethren, let us bear all things with patience and resignation, knowing that men are not to be our judges; let us be sincerely thankful for the late revival of God's work among us, and steadily cherish the same and be steadfast, unmovable, always abounding in the work of the Lord, all the powers of darkness will be engaged to check this glorious work; and one thing will certainly be aimed at, and that will be to draw your attention to other subjects, and if possible to keep you from suitable engagements for the salvation of precious souls. The instruments that God makes use of in carrying on his work will be as marks for the enemy to shoot at from every quarter. But if we keep our eye fixed on the Savior they can do us no harm, but will often unintentionally do us good. For my own part I can truly say these things have sometimes been a great comfort to me; and when reproaches and slanders have been flying, thick on every side, my soul has been happily feasting on the love of God and a spirit to pity and pray for my persecutors, and sometimes my friends have thought that I should certainly be overwhelmed. I could still say with Paul that none of these things move me, neither count I my life as dear to myself. So that I may finish my course with you and the ministry, and that I may have received the Lord Jesus to testify the Gospel of the Grace of God. Again I say with the same servant of God, after the way they call heresy so worship I the God of my fathers believing all things that are written in the law and the prophets.

And now, brethren, I commend you to God, and the word of his grace, which is able to build you up, and give you an inheritance among all them that are sanctified. The grace of our Lord Jesus Christ be with you all. Amen.

I am your servant,
For Jesus' sake,
John Mulkey

A History of the Mill Creek ("Old Mulkey") Church
Tompkinsville, Kentucky

Appendix B

Mill Creek Church Minutes 1798-1807

(B-2)

Covenant

On account of the various opinions now abounding among the professors of christianity concerning covenants, we the subscribers believe the practice to be scriptural from the following passages of scriptures viz. Josh. 24th 25... 2 Chron. 15, 8 & 14 Neh. 9 & 38 Jer. 50 ...

We believe also to be a necessary duty for the comfort & well being of us as a church to ... hold forth ... the following articles.

... baptism by immersion, laying ... election of Grace by the predestination... Jesus, effectual calling by ... the imputed righteousness ... sanctification thro' Gods grace & ... final perseverance of the saints in grace the resurrection ... after death life everlasting.

... one living & true God to be our God, ... the Father, the Son & the Holy ghost ...

(B-3)

& partake the scriptures of the [...]
to be the revealed mind & will of
[...] the aid of the Spirit to make them
our faith & practice & to be [gov...]
church discipline — We do acknowledge [...]
children of wrath by nature & our [...]
God is only thro' the imputed righteousness
apprehended & received by faith alone we do promise [...]
each other weakness & infirmities with much [...]
not discovering them to any out [...]
But by gospel order as in matthew 18:15, 16, 17 [...]
of the like nature We believe God acts as sovereign
of all things our souls our bodies & all we have [...]
is at his sovereign disposal under every act of [...]
in every circumstance of life we should be ready [...]
to him as such & do purpose thro' the aid of [...]
So to do believing it will be most for the glory of God [...]
mutual comfort of each other we do [...]
of divine grace unitedly give up our selves to each
other as Brethren in Christ

Old Mulkey: A Pioneer Plea for the Ancient Order

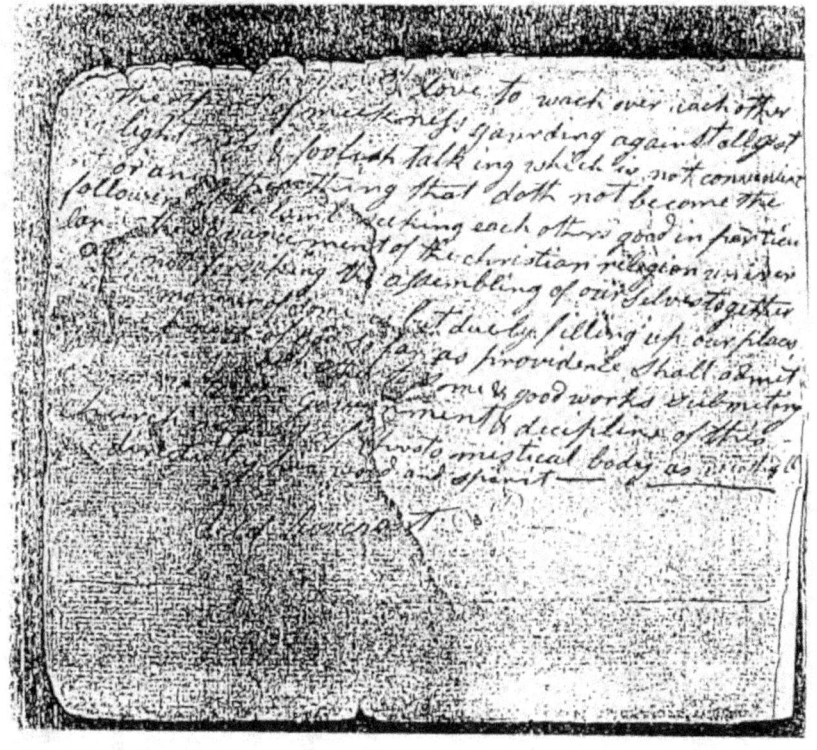

(B-5)

(B-6)

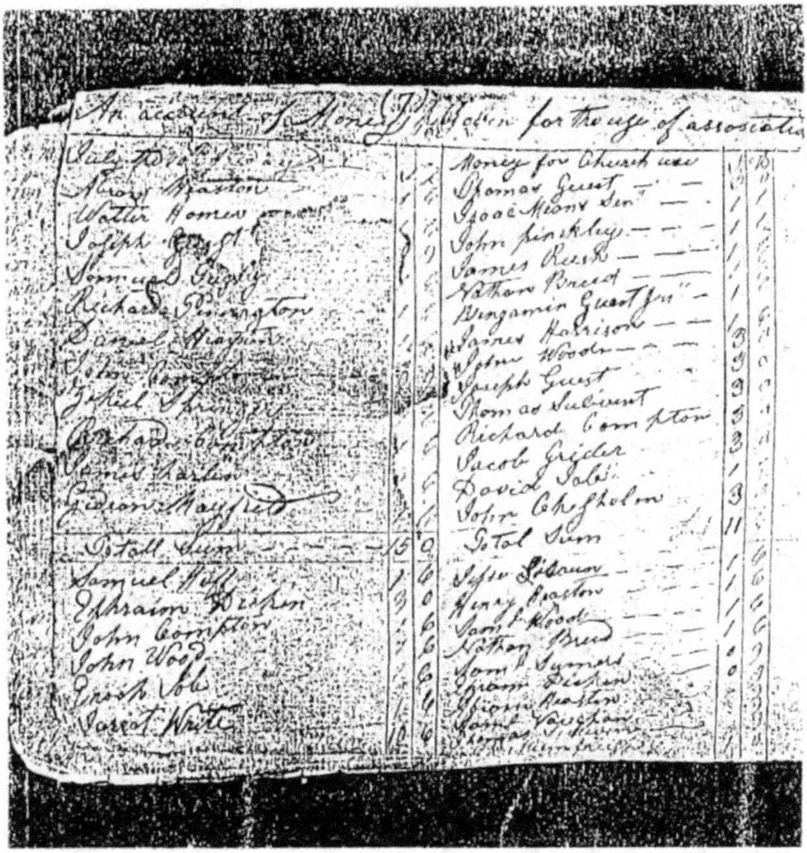

> (8)
>
> Sept 11th 1798
> Church Met at Harlans and after divine
> worship proceeded to Business as follows
> 1st John and Nancy Compton Joind By Letter
> and Bartholomew Wood By Living tes=
> =tamony —
> 2nd petitioned for helps To ordain church
> officers to attend next meeting
> 3rd Jno Mulkey and John Wood Chosen dele=
> =gates to the asso.n
> 4th Adjourned till next meeting in Course
>
> October 13th 1798 Church met at at the meeting
> house and after divine worship proce=
> =ed to Business
> 1st the minutes of the asso.n read and agreed
> to

> October 15 1798
> 2nd after some examination the church ag[reed]
> to appoint and set forward Philip
> Mulkey to the work [of] a dea[con]
> 3 Concluded that the members are to ap-
> propriat money to be lodged in the
> deacons hand for the use of the church
> 4th adjourned till meeting in course —
>
> Nov. Church did not meet
>
> Dec. Did not meet
>
> January 12th 1799
> Church met and after prayer proceed
> to business
> 1st received by experience Ezekiel & Rebek[ah]
> Springer and Nancy Gurr
> Nathan Baird

> January 2 Brother Ino Wood apointed elder of this
> Church
> 3rd Adjournd till next meting
>
> Feb 9th 1739
> Church met and after worship proceed
> 2d to business
> 1st conferd on some matters and —
> Adjournd till next meeting
>
> March 9th 1739
> Church met and after prayer proceded
> to business
> 1st 3 joind by Letter Morgret Aston —
> Hannah Perington Susanah Cummins
> 2 a complaint laid against Brother —
> Enoch Job for being intoxicated with
> liquor and he suspended from prevelige
> and

> April 13 1799
>
> 4 Thos Sulivant and Philip Mulkey appointed to cite him to next church meeting
> 3 adjourned till next meeting
> 1 as Enoch Job did not attend the matter was postponed till next meeting for a satisfaction
> 2nd the church agree to commune 3 times in the year may July & october.
> 3rd the church agree to meet stated on church meeting days at eleven oclock and also to have preaching before the Church sits to do business
> 4th adjourn'd till meeting in course
>
> May 11th 1799
>
> Church met according to adjournment and after divine Service proceeded to business
> As brother Enoch Job did not attend the matter respecting him was again referred till next meeting

> 2 The church grant a certificate to Brother
> Jno. Mulkey in order for him to obtain
> license to marry
> 3 Adjourned till till the 2nd Saturday in
> June

June 9th 1799
> The church met and after worship proceeded
> to business —
> 1st Brother Enoch Key came forward and
> satisfaction being given he was rec'd to
> 2nd Adjourned till the 2nd friday in
> July —

July 12 1799
> Church met — the accounts lost or said
> At present.

August
> Minutes Lost — —

> 1799
> Sept
> oct
> 10ber   All
>   Lost
>
> Jan.3   Church met & after worship proceed
> 7th   to business
> 1800   1 door being opened Elisabeth Wood
>   Joined by experience
>   2 the Church Looking on it is a
>   duty for all heads of familys to main
>   tain the worship of god in their family
>   appointed Brethren Benjamin gist &
>   John Ino Mulkey to visit all the
>   members of this church to enquire
>   how they do & stir them up to duty
>   adjourned till next meeting

(B-15)

> Feby 8th 1800 Church met and after prayer proceded to business.
> 1 Jarret Wright joind by Letter
> 2 the church appoint Brethren to invite out lying members to come & see us, — and give their reasons for not joining
>
> March 8th 1800 the Church Met — &c.
> 1 by Letter recievd
> Dd Harlan & wife David Job & Wife
> Saml Vaughan Daniel Heestand
> Jno Maddox & wife & Emund Wade
> 2 the Church considerd of the Lords day & thought a reformation necessary

(B-17)

(16)

May 9th 1800 — Church met acording to adjournment & after prayer proceded to business
1. a door being opened for the reception of members Isbel Bishong joind by letter
2. Call'd Bro. Benjamin Gist to the office of Elder in this Church he having been previously ordaind
3rd Agreeably to a former appointment the church agree to have for 2nd Elder no good set apart to the office of elder by ordination
4. The Church agree for Bro. Philip Mulkey & Jos. Gist to be set apart to the office of deacon by ordination
5th —

(17)

5 the Church do agree to send br ministerial helps in or to install their Minister at their July meeting & make Brt Jno Wood their messenger

6 Adjourned &c

May 31st of Jun. — Church met and after divine worship proceeded to business

1 A door being opened for the reception of members Sarah Morris joined by letter

2 the Church appoint Bro. Jno Mulkey Benjn Gist senr Jno Wood & Jos July to attend a conference held on Beaver creek the 1st Saturday in June

Adjourned &c

July
term
1800

(18)
2nd saturday
Church Met and Bro. Charles Jarvit
& Robt. Smith came forward accord
to the churches request for the installa.
of their minister
1 the ministeriel helps enquiring is it
the churches duty to suport the
Minister the church answers it
2 does the minister think it his duty
not only to preach statedly But
occasionally & to visit the Sick &c
he agrees it is upon which
3rd he is pronounced their minister &
the church the people of his charge

> August term 1800
>
> 2nd Saturday ('19)
> the Church met and after prayr proceeded to business as follows —
> 1st a door opend for the reception of membrs Ephraim Ellis came forward and joined by experience
> 2nd
> dr John Maddox and wife were dismissd
> Adjourned &c
>
> Septem term 1800
>
> 2nd Saturday
> The Church met and after worship proceded to business as follows —
> 1st James Sedlock excommunicated for the sin of fornication &c
> 2nd five joind the Church three by exp

Sept
1800
2D
Saturday

...rience and two by letter (20)

3rd Requests from Churches on pitmans Creek and in Russels settlement complyd with. this Church gives up her pasture the first and third sunday in every month. to attend them Churches

4th the Church apointed brother John Mulkey to attend an association held in Cumberland the fourth saturday in September

5th they appointed brethren John Mulkey Benjamin Gist Ino. Wood and Thomas Sulivant to attend an association held on Little barron the 1st saturday in november 1800

> (21) the Church appoint brethren Thomas sul=
> vant Nathan Breed and James Ha[r]
> land to form a plan for the support of
> Minister
>
> October 1800 — adjourn'd till meeting in course
>
> November
> December
> January
> February
> March
>
> Minutes and transactions of this Meeting All lost ----
>
> All mislaid
>
> April 1801 — Saturday 11th the Church met and after Divine worship proceed to business as follows
> 1st a door opened for the reception of members

two Came forward and join'd by letter Abraham (22)
Weston and Rebekah Wiley Ragina More
2nd Adjourn'd till meeting in course

May 9 1801

The Church met and after worship proceed to business as follows —

1st a door open'd for the reception of members
6 six came forward and join'd by experience
Rebekah Job James Rush Gideon Mayfield
2nd Molley Rush Nancy Welch Jane Proctor
Margret Killey join'd by letter and
3rd Mourning Denton by bareing testomony
4th James Tadlock restor'd to his seat
5th Adjourn'd till meeting in course

Old Mulkey: A Pioneer Plea for the Ancient Order

13th June 1801 — Church met and after divine worship proceed to business as follows
1st a door opend for the reception of members by letter three came forward and joined Saphia Sims Francis Ray then by experience came forward and joind Robert Kirkby Miles Haley Jas Clerk Fanny Wood Sally Baleys Franky Scott Sarah Silvcant Richard Smith Isaac Means Thomas Wiley John Pinkly Ruth Holmes John Denton Christian

15 Fraily Walter Holmes
2nd adjourn'd till the last Saturday this instant

June 27, 1801 Saturday — The Church appointed Bethren Jn Mulkey, Benjamin Guyet & Jn Wood and Thomas Sulurn to attend association on Barren three Jekiel Springer James Harlin & Phillip Mulkey call to Exer: three gift of Exortation within the Church

(24)

July 10 friday 1801

" the Church met according to adjournment & after prayer proceeded to business as fol
1st a committee of seven members was chosen to settle a matter of difficulty with Saml. moss and their decision was to be final the committee report they discover no signs of repentence and he is excld for contending for unsound principles & the like
2nd a matter respecting Jas Sadlock & Edmnd wade was consider.d and wade confessing the act of adultry was excluded for the same and Brother Sadlock was acquited
3rd on Saturday a door was open'd for the reception of members and 3 Joind by letter and 15 by experience

15

4 adjourn'd till next meeting the 1st Saturday in August

(25)

Saturday August 1st 1801

The Church Met and after Divine Service Proceeded to Business as follows Viz —
A door open for the Reception of Members Then Came forward and Joind by Experience Poley Ray — Kibby Kirby. Rebkoh Denton Thomas Wood. Barsheba Nelson — Abrom denton Isaac Denton: Joel Nelson: Grace Rueff Thomas Ray: Sally Nelson: Thomas Gueff Thomas Welch — — —
Adjourned to the 2nd Saturday In September —

September 12th 1801 Saturday

Church Met and after prayer proceeded to Business As follows —
1st Church Covenants Read and a query arising Concerning laying on of hands thought proper to Make Search for Satisfaction and Make Report next Meeting In Course as also Some other alterations therein thought nesasary

September 12 1801 Saturday

2d A Door opened for the (No 6) Reception of Members — And 3 Came forward and Joined by letter — And 12 by Experience —

3d A petition came forward from the Church on Kettle Creek for helps on purpose of ordination & Comply with & appointed Brethren. John Mulkey, John Wood, Benjamin Guest Sinr. Joseph Guest and Philip Mulkey to attend the 4th Saturday In this Instant

4th Phillip Mulkey about to take a journey applys for License to Exercise his gift and Complyd with

5th Joseph Bailes Colld to Exercise his Gift within the Bounds of the Church — — — Adjourned

Sept 13 1801 Sunday

A Door opend for the Reception of Members then Came forward and Joind by Experience. Adjournd till the 4th Saturday In this Instant A Day Appointed for Church Business

(27)

September 24th 1801 Friday — Church Met and after Prayer proceeded to Business
1st William Wood, and Sarah Wood his wife Joind by letter — — — —
2nd An accusation Brought forward against Giles Kelley for having a wife In Carolina —
Him and his wife suspended from priviledges till The Certainty Can be had — — — — —
3rd Samuel Frogley desired a letter of Dismission Granted
Adjourned till Meeting In Course 2nd Saturday October

October 10th Saturday — Church Met and after Prayer Proceeded as follows
1st A door opined for Reception of Members & Joind
2nd the Refference of the Church Covenant considered the article of Laying on of hands Disanulld
3rd A letter Sent by Jas Cook to The Church Concerning his wifes having another husband yet alive —
The Church Refferss it till nex Meeting In Cours
4th A petition from Mudcamp Church for helps In a presbitery for the Restoration of R. Smith to the Ministry Comply'd Send Brethren Jn Wood William Wood Benj Guist & Jn Compton

(28)

October 10th Saturday

5th A Difficulty being between Nancy Gunn & Kibby Kirby the Church appoint Joshua & Ja Harlen to labour with them for Reconciliation and make Report next Meeting &c

6th Considered of Communion agreed to Commence but twice In the year Viz May & October Ensuing

7th William Wood Call to Exercise his Gift of the Ministry & Adjourned till Meeting In Course

November 7th 801 Saturday

Church Met and after Divine Service proceeded &c
1st Door opend for Reception of Members none Came
2nd The Refference Concerning Jos Clark been added And the Church asking him to be present Before they proceed to Any thing final — Order the Clerk to Cite them by writing to Attend next Meeting In Course

3rd Harlen Report that Labours used & fellowship Regaind Between Sister Gunn & Sister Kirby

(B-30)

Continued
November
7th 1801
Saturday   4ly The Church appoint Saturday 21st of this m[onth]
A Day of fasting and prayer —
Adjourned till 12 December Saturday

December
12
1801
Saturday   Church Met and after Divine Service proceded as follows
1st A Door opened for the Reception of Members & Come forw[ard]
2nd James Clark and wife Being present the Refference
Concerning this way the live considered and the Church
finding them to be living In adultry, They were Exclud[ed]
from fellowship with us —
3rd The Church agrees to Make up Some provisions
Such as Corn and pork for the Support of —
Brother John Mulkey —
4th Sammuel Harris Request a Second hearing
This Church appoints them a Comittee of Six Members
Viz Saml Summers Jarret White Robt Kirby
Thomas Welch Rd Guest & Jo Bacls attend on
Tuesday 22nd of this Instant at the Meeting hous[e]
With hers and their testmany on Each party to
Reason in this Matter and Make Report to x
Meting In Course.

(B-31)

(B0)

December 12th 1801 Saturday
Phillip Mulkey Aplyd for Relieusement from the Work of Deacon --- Granted ------
Adjourned till 9th of January 1802 Saturday

January 9th 1802 Saturday
Church Met and after Divine Service proceeded as follows Vz - 1st a door opend for Reception of Members And 4 Joind by Letter - - -
2nd the Refference Conserning Saml Mars Calld for the Committee Report they Believe Injure Done to him Heretofore a final Dicision Is Therfore Made By the Church Concerning this Matter
3rd Obadiah Howard Calld to the work of a Deacon In this Church Being previously ordained
4th thought propper to Inlarge the Meeting henesoxe Agree to Consider of a plan for the proceeding To That Business and Settled on the Method Next Meeting In House ------
5th By agreement of the Church Any Male Member of this Church having Affair Church Meeting they Shall Come forward at

(B-32)

January Saturday 1802	Church Met and after prayer proceeded to Business 1 Received Nicholas and Jean Dowses and Philip Briant James Chapman & Robert Lane and Mary By Letter, 2 Sister green came forward and Talkd to the Church the Church agree to wait with her till another Meeting adyournd &c
February Saturday 1802	Church Met and after prayer proceeded to Business 1 the Reference Concerning sister green the church agree to wait yet to another Meeting, 2 Received peter Jackson and Margret by letter 3 Received Brother John Roden In full feloship 4 The Church Appoint a Committy of five members John wood obadiah howard James Warland Thomas Sulavant & John Cumpston to see what is lacking of Being made up for the support of the ministry and to lay a plan for making up the Balance and make return next meeting

Continued
Jan 9th
1802
Saturday

the Nft and assign their reasons for not attending and that Missing too together they shall be Inveted By a Messenger from the Church ——
Ajourned till Saturday 13th Febuary 1802 —

February
13th
Saturday
1802

Church Met and after Divine Service proceded Viz 1st Petition from Mudcam Church for helpe In Order to Reconsider of Robert Smith Being Restord to the Ministry the Church agree to Send Brethren John Mulkey Phillip Mulkey Benjamin Guest Senr & John Wood to attend them 4th Saturday In March ——
2nd Door opend for Reception of Members s Joining by letter And the Refrence Concerning the Meeting house Dropt or laid over till a futur Period Ajournd to 13th March Saturday —

March
13th
1802
Saturday

Church Met and after Singing and prayer Proceded to Business as follows Viz 1st Door opend for Reception of Members Joind by letter Viz Mary Green ——
2d Brethren Saml Vaughen and Danl Hearten

> Continued
> March 13th
> Saturday
> 1802
>
> (132)
> Were Ordered by the Church to Cite Brother Joel Nelson to Attend Next Meeting In course —
> 3rd Brother Henry Heartin having for Several Meetings Withdrawn himself from his seat In the Church Brethren John Mulkey Obadiah Howard & Benjamin Guest Sen.r are appointed to use Labours with him and Know his Reason for So doing —
> 4th The Church agree that their be a Church Meeting held at Abram Dentons Sen.r Saturday 20 of this Month —
> Adjourned till 20th of April Saturday
>
> March 20th 1802
> Saturday
>
> Church Met at Abram Dentons and after Divine Services proceeded as follows Viz
> 1st Phillip Mulkey Chosen Moderator —
> 2nd A Door opened for the Reception of Members then came forward & joined Joined by Experience —
> 3 Peggy Gregg & Elizah Denton & Abram Denton by Reanimation —
> Adjourned &c —

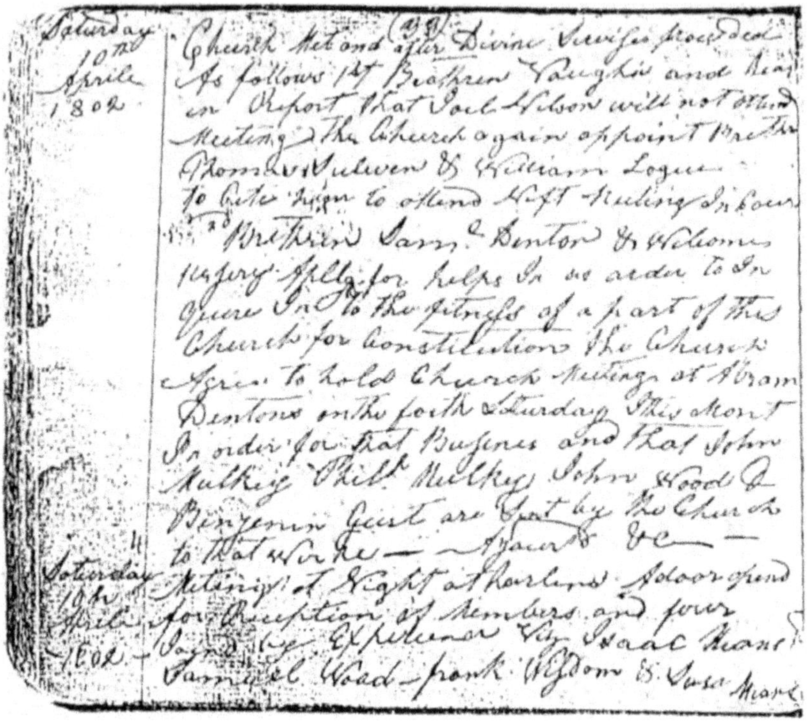
Saturday 10th Aprile 1802 — Church Met and (93) after Divine Service proceeded
As follows 1st Brethren Vaughn and [illegible]
in Report that Joel Wilson will not attend
Meeting the Church again appoint Brethren
Thomas Sulivan & William Logue
to Cite him to attend Next Meeting in Course
2nd Brethren Saml. Denton & Welcome
Ussery Apply for helps in an order to In
quire In to the fitness of a part of the
Church for Constitution the Church
Agree to hold Church Meeting at Abram
Dentons on the forth Saturday this Mont
In order for that Business and that John
Mulkey Phil. Mulkey John Wood &
Benjamin Gist are Sent by the Church
to that Worke — Signed &c —
Saturday 10th Aprile 1802 — Meeting at Night at Harlins A door opend
for Reception of Members and four
Joind by Experience Viz Isaac Mans
Samuel Wood - frank Wisdom & Susa Mark

> **Friday 1802**
>
> (34) Church Met and after Divine Service proceded as follows 1st ty Door opened for Reception of Members then come forward and by Letter Joel Noor & Carr & Rachel Springer by Experience Thomas Coe under the W. Care of the as full fellowship by Gospell order Adjournd &
>
> **Saturday June 12 1802**
>
> Church Met and after Divine Service proceded as follows 1st Brother Joel Nelson come forward And Acknowledged that his Difficultis are Re_____ and he Is Restord to his Seat — 2d The Church Consider of the Circumstances of Brother Siles Killie and wife and no testimony being Brought forward to Authinticate the Charge laid Again them they are Restored again to the of this Church 3 A Door opend for Reception of Members And 3 Joind by letter and 2 by Experience — 4 A Letter from a part of this Church on Mill Creek South of Cumberland River for helps In order to Inquire Into there fittness for Constitution

(35)

Saturday 12 June 1802

Agree to Answer them next Meeting In Course
5th A letter from Roring River Church concerning Brother Roden he Is Suspended from privilidge till further Examination be Made
6 Apointed Brethren John Mulkey Benjamin Guist And Obadiah Howard to Atend The association At this place last Saturday In July 1802
—— Adjourd &c ———

Sunday 10th July 1802

Church Met and after Preaching proceded as follows
1st The Church Give up part of the Church South of Cumberland River for Constitution It found fit when a Presbetry for that purpose is Aforesaid — 2nd Apoint Benjamin Guist &c to use private labours with the Roring River Brethren Respecting Br Roden for Satisfaction 3 Agree to have Monthly Meeting Stated by Second Saturday In Every Month
2 Adjourned

> Saturday August 14th 1802
>
> Church Met and after prayer proceedid as folows 1st Brother John Mulky Being absent Brother Phillep Mulky Chosen Moderator 2nd A Door opend for Reception of Members Recievd by Experience Lidia Vaughan 3rd Apointed Brethren Thomas Sulwon Saml Vaughan & Abram Heastin To use Labours with James Green and wife for Recomittation and Make Report Next Meeting In Course 4th Binjomin Denton Aplyd for a leter of Dismission for him & Wife Granted A Dismission Granted for Rachel Cole Being Removd out of the Bounds of this Church Francess Wisdom About to Take a Journey Aplyd for a letter of Recommindation Granted Adjourned &c
>
> Sunday Morning a Door opend for Ofsers Recievd James Green Junr

> September
> 2d Saturday
> 1802
>
> Church Met and after Divine Service
> Proceeded to Business as follows 1st Brother
> John Mulkey being absent Brother Phillip
> Mulkey Chosen Moderator for the present &
> and the Church Appoint Brother [illegible] [illegible]
> to cite Brother Joseph Writer to Attend Next
> meeting the Courosy.
> Appoint Brethren [illegible] [illegible] and Gideon
> Mayfield to cite Brother Samuel Summers
> to attend Next Meeting Adjourned. &c

> Octr
> 2nd Saturday
> 1802
>
> 1 Brother Samuel Summers Come forward and
> acknowledged his wrong and the Church
> admit him again to a seat ——
> 2 Brs Joseph Wright came forward and by
> his acknowledgement is still retained in
> felowship —— 3 the reference concerning
> Bro Wroden taken up the Church ap[point]
> that Brethren Benjamin Gist John
> Wood Obediah Howard Thos [Gist]
> want John Mulkey Wm [illegible]
> Joseph Gist [illegible]

Old Mulkey: A Pioneer Plea for the Ancient Order

a comettie from this church to meet Capt
Hamiltons on mill Creek on the 3rd friday in
December also that we petition Brimstone
Church for helps and that we call for roaring
River Church to authenticate the charge
against Bro Wooden also call for Salem Church
in the same
4 Brother Thos Caron formerly a man under
the watch care of this Church was received
in full fellowship ———
Query ——— 5 a charge being laid in again
Brother Wm Hoff for having unbecoming
Behavior appointed Broth Thos Gist Thos
Welch to cite him to attend next meeting
in course
6 The church appointed Bren Thos Jubin
Saml Vaughan & abram Hiestand to Labor
with sister Green and also to cite her
to next meeting to give satisfaction for
her errors 7 appoint Bro Jiles Kelley to
invite Bro Othos Wood to attend next meet
in course

(39)

8 Jas Green & Jesse Jobe applyed for Letters of Deomfsion Granted Adjourned &c

Nov 13 Saturday 1802 — Saturday Church Met and after prayer 1 The Brethren appointed to Labour with sister green Report that they gained no satisfaction But She not attending the church agrees to wait with her till Next Meeting, 2 Wm Huff Came forward And gave general Satisfaction and is restored To his seat, 3. The Members on wards Branch given up to be constituted an arm of This Church & Sarah Judah and Jos Wright David Lisaun and Rebekah Jobe and James Cole dismissd Adjourned &c.

December Saturday 1802 — 1 Received Brother Hopkin Stephen Howard By Letter Adjourned &c

March Saturday 1803. Church Met and after prayr proceded To Business 1 Goshua MPerson Came forward and was Received By Letter, 2 Received Ambrose gibs Under the watch Cair of this Church. 3 The Reference Concerning Sister green She Is Restored to her Seat Again ——— 4 Sister Margret Aften applyd for a letter of Dismission, granted Adgournd ()

Aprile 2th Saturday 1803 Church Met and after prayer proceeded as follows 1st Sister Nancy welch Excluded for withdrawing from the Church.

2nd Brother John Mulkey Sit at liberty to go wheresoever he May think proper —

3rd Diug Does The Church In The Doctrine of the Trinity, as sets forth In the Confession of faith. Answer. yes —

> Query Can we hold any In fellowship that Do not Believe the Same
> Answer No
> Brother Nathan Breed Appointed to Cite Samuel Summers to attend Next Meeting
> Adjourned &c. &c.

May 13th Saturday 1803
> Church Met and after Worship provided &c A Door opend for Reception of Members Received by Letter Brother Francis Baxter and Mary Baxter his wife Consulted on Several Matters and Adjourn

June 11 Saturday 1803
> Church Met and after Sermon Proceded to Business 1st Brother Henry Heaton Having for Some time withdrawn himself from a Seat among us Appointed Brethren Joseph Guest

> June 11 Saturday 1803
>
> Thomas Sulevent and Samuel Vaughn to use labours with him for S[...] And Make Report Next Meeting In Course 2nd A Door opned for Reception of Mem brs Recevd by Experience Betsy Bradley Susana Buster 3rd Apointed Broth" John Mulkey Thomas Sulevent &c Joseph Guest to Attend the Asso: At Mou"t Gilead 1st Satter In July

> July 9th Saturday 1803
>
> Church Met and after prayer proceded as follows — 1st Brother Henry Heaster being present but Refusing To hear the Church & Withdrawing himself from the Church He Is therefore Excluded from fellowship Among us — 2nd Petition from Concord for Helps

> The Church agree to Send Brethren
> Jn Mulkey Mozs Guest Jn Wood Obed Howard
> Franz Baxter Chris Bailey Eper Springer &c
> Ja Harlin To Attend on the 1st Saturday
> In August The Church appoint Brethren
> Daniel Hensten and John Compton
> to Cite Frank Wisdom to Attin next
> Meeting In Course Adjourn'd

August 13th Saturday 1803

> Church Met and after Sermon proceeded &c
> 1st The Reference Respecting Bro Wisdom laid over
> 2nd Bro Thomas Wood Aplyes for Dismission Granted
> 3rd Br. Isaac Means Junr Set at liberty to
> Exersise his Gift within the Bouns of this the
> Brimstone Church —
> Recvd by Experience Betsy howard & by
> Letter John Powel Adjourn'd &c —

(B-46)

> Sept 10th 1803 Saturday
>
> Church Met and after prayer proceeded &c A Door opend for Reception of Members Received by letter Mary Demint Also by letter Elizabeth Rebekah and Betsy Brown Appointed Brethren Ephraim Ellis and Thorn as [wulet] to [Bro] Joseph Write to them Next Meeting In course

> October term friday 1803
>
> Church Met and after Divine Service Proceded as follows Viz 1st the Refference Respecting Bro Francess Wisdom Called for the Brethren Report that by good Information He lives a very Disorderly life And Refuseth to hear the Call of this Chur And we Therefore Declare a Nonfellowship with him — 2d Tho W. Brethren appointed to [bite] Joseph Writs Report that He also Refuseth to hear the Church And we Therefore Declare a Nonfellowship With him

> 3rd Some things In our church covenant
> thought Nesesary to be erased and to
> alter the language of the articles of
> the the Green River association agreed
> to Consider of it to Next Meeting In doars
> A Door open for the Reception of Members
> Received by letter John Sumers and wife
> by Experience John Condra Received
> Poley Got by being testimony also Reba
> Cons In the same Maner — Br
> Giles Killis laid under Suspention
> Brethren Thompkins and Wm Sadel
> Desired letters of Dismission Granted
> A Door open for Reception of Members
> Received by Experence Christopher Dove
> Wm Howard and Wm Sumers —
> Adjourned &c —

Saturday October [torn]

November
Town
Saturday
1803

Church Met and after prayer Proceeded &c
The Reference Respecting the Church Covenant
laid over 2nd A Door opend for Reception
of Members Received by letter Sarah Conete

December
2nd
Saturday
1803

Church Met and after prayer proceeded &c
1st The Reference Concerning the Church
Covenant Still laid over —
2nd The Church appoint Brethren Joseph
Gist Francis Baxter & Robert Kerbys to
Labour with Sister Lidia Marrs for her
Satisfaction and Make Report next Meeting
3rd Appointed Brother Thomas Gist To Invite
Bro Laban Ellis to attend Next Meeting

January
14th
1804
Saturday

Church Met and after prayer proceded &c
1st The Reference Concerning the Church Covna,
Calld for This Church apoint Brethren —
John Mulkey Benjamen Gist senr John
Wood —

January
term
Continued

Obadiah Howard Francess Baxter a Committee to arange Matter and present at Next Meeting In Course
1st The Refrence Respecting Sister Mars laid over
3rd The Refrence Respecting Br. Laban Ellis Cauld for & The Church again appoint Brother Benjamin Gist & Thomas Welch To Labour With him & Make Report Next Meeting
4th Brother Josephs Bailes Declaring a Nonfellowship with himself and withdrawing himself from the Church we Say therefore that he Is no more of us
5th A Request for a letter of Dismission for John Powel Granted — Adjournd &c.

february
11-1804
Saturday

Church Met &c — The Refrence Respecting Cauld for The Church ____ addapt The Stitution of the green river association with some perticulars added thereunto

(B-50)

> Febuary Term Continued
>
> The Church agree and Say that any Member of this Church Having Refused to Meetings that be Called for to give her Reasons for not attending The Brother appointed to Cite Laban Eller to attend this Meeting Report that he Intirely Refuses to hear the Cals of this Church and we therefore Say that he Is no More of us ———
> The Reference Respecting Lidia Marrs Called for And She being present and declaring a non-fellowship with the Church She Is therefore Excluded from from fellowship among us A door opened for Reception of Members ——
> Received by letter Polly Ward & Phebe Gore —
>
> March 10th 1804 Saturday
>
> Church Met And after prayer Proceeded A door opened for Reception of Members ——
> Received by Experience Sally wood John Compton Aplyed for Dismission for himself and wife Also Elijah Denton Aplyed for Dismission gran. Thomas Bar having often and publickly transgresed and no Signs of Repentence appearing We Say therefore that he Is no More of us —

> March
> Term
> Continued
> 1804
>
> Brother Samuel Huff having been long absent from the Church Appointed Brethren John Mulkey and Thomas Guest to cite him to attend Next Meeting In Course. Appointed Brethren Ephraim Ellis and Benjamin Guest Junr. to cite Thomas Wood Junr. to attend next Meeting
>
> April
> 12th
> Saturday
> 1804
>
> Church Met and after Prayer Proceeded & 1st Door opend for Reception of Members Received by letter Nancy Radford, by Experience Tilman Crow Rosilly Grider Polley Carr the Reference Respecting Bro Saml Huff Calld for and he being present and giving Satisfaction he Is again Restored to a Seat. ———
> Also Bro Thos Wood being Present and acknowleding his Wrongs He Is Retaind amongst us — Appointed a Committee of Seven Members viz John Wood Nathan Bruce Jos Harlow Ephraim Ellis Francess Baxter Joseph Guest & Thomas Sulevin at this place on the 28th of this April to fix a plan for Building a Meetinghouse

> **May 11th 1804 Friday** — Church Met and after Prayer Proceeded &c. The Committee Report that the Meeting house Is to be 50 feet long 30 wide Shingled with Joint Shingles 5 windows and three Door A man to be hired to Build It and paid In trade by Subscription — Aprobated Opind A Door for Reception of Members — Received by Experience Christopher Grider And Francy & Brother Thompson o dec Gave up his letter agreed to the Church The Church a gree to Consider of Publick fasting & Converce thereon next Meeting
>
> **Saturday May 18** — At the Stage Revived by Experience Polley Dickeson Polley Strowd by letter Juda White Henry King Elizabeth King Nancy —
>
> **June Tenth Saturday 1804** — Church Met &c A Door open for Reception of Members Received by Experience William Chism & Nancy Thompson by letter Nancy Soh

> Appointed Brethren John Mulkey, Joseph Gist
> And Isaac Means Jun.r to attend the association
> at Sinking creek Creek
> Appointed Brother Samuel Vaughan Daniel
> heasten to Cite Sister Green to next Meeting
> The Ruperence Respecting Silas Kelley Called
> for And It being Athenticly prooved that
> his first wife Is yet a live we therefore
> Say that him and the woman he now
> lives with Is no more of us ———
>
> July Church Met & after Sermon proceded &c
> June A Door opened for Reception of Members
> 1802 Received by Experience Jacob Chism &
> Pricilla Chism his wife Letter to the
> Association Read and approved ———
> James Baxter Received by Experience
> And Nancy Clerk — Adjourned

(B-54)

> August
> 4th
> Saturday
> 1804
>
> Church Met &c — ther Reference Respecting publick
> Fasting Calld for — the Church agree that publick
> fasting May bee attended to In Case of publick
> Cale matters In Church or State
> The Church having In possion a Dismision letter
> Belonging to Stephen Lowards negro Girl pig
> And She never aplying for fellowship
> Appointed Brethren John Wood & Robt Kerby
> to labour with her and Know her reasons
> & make Report next mating In Course —
> Appointed a publick fast on tho morrow —
>
> Sept 2t
> 1804
> Saturday
>
> Church Met & after Sermon proceded &c —
> Minutes of the association Brought forward
> the Reference Respecting pig Calld for
> And She Being present askd the matter being
> Canceld the Church Delare a non fellowship
> With her — The Reference Respecting Sister
> Green Calld for and being present & giving
> Satisfaction She Is Restored to a Seat —
> William Hust Excluded for Immoral Conduct

Saturday September 28th 1804	Church Met &c — Some Conference held concerning the Covnant & Rules of Decorum the Covnant Still Retains
October 12-1804 Friday	Church Met &c — Some matters of Difficulty Existing Between Bro Wm Summers Isom Hay & Isaac Means Appointed Brethren John Mulkey Benjn Gist Jno Wood Francis Baxter Joseph Gist Ezekial Springer Jas Harlen & Jacob Grider with the agreed Brethren to meet at this place on Friday 2nd November next to Labour for Satisfaction
October 13th Saturday 1804	Church Met &c — A charge being found against Brother Jas Harrison appointed Brethren Baxter Harlen Springer & Benjn Gist Sent to Labour with him & make Report Next Meeting Appointed Brother Baxter to Cite Robt Cade to attend next meeting —

> November
> 10th
> Saturday
> 1804
>
> Church Met &c – The Reference Respecting Brother Harrison called for the Committee Report that Satisfaction Is given the Is Therefore Retained — In fellowship ————
> The Reference Respecting Brethren Hayse Mean and Summers Call for the Committee Report that no Satisfaction Is given And Summers Being absent ~~————~~ Is deferred till next Meeting & appointed Brother Gilder to bear him to Attend — The Church agree that they will Make up the Ballance of what Cannot be made up by Subscription when the Meeting House Is Compleated by Iles Thompson or Swagin A letter of dismission Granted to Joppa Sims
>
> December
> Term
> 1804
>
> Church Met &c The Reference Respecting Bro W. Summers Called for & he not coming forward but Refusing to hear the Church A nonfellowship Is declared with him — The Matter Respecting Robt Lane Refd David &c ——

> **January 19th 1805 Saturday**
> Church Met &c. The Refference Respecting Robt Cane Called for and Being present and appearing to Still be Regardless of the crimes wherewith he was Charged the Church Say that he Is no more of us — a charge laid In against Thomas wood for Reppeted Trensagresions the Church Say that He Is no more one of us Adjourn &c

> **February 9th 1805 Saturday**
> Church Met &c Appointed Brethren Saml Vaughan & Wm Logue to Cite Br Baxter to attend Next Meeting A door opend for Reception of Members Received By Letter John Springer & Wife Mary Springer & Mary Springer Junr & Dianah Anderson Cold Brother Porter to the office of Deacon In this Church

> **March 9th 1805 Saturday**
> Church Met &c The Reffrence Respecting Br Baxter Calld for & He Being present & Giving publick Satisfaction he Is Restored To a Seat Wm Jomes taken under the watch care of the Church Receivd by Experience Nancy Houser ———— Turn over

> **March 9th**
> **Continued**
> A difficulty existing between Brother Abram Hearten & wife of the one part & Sister Mary Green of the other. Appointed Brethren John Woods Jo Gist And Jas Harlin to labour with them for reconciliation & Make Report Next Meeting. In course also cite them to be present at that time
>
> **April 13 1805 Saturday**
> Church Met & after Sermon Proceeded as follows A Door opened for Reception of Members Received by Experience William Cohorn Peggy Yorke the Reference concerning Brr Hearten & Sister Green Called for the Committee Report That no Reconciliation & all Being Present & the Matter being fairly Considered the Church Say that Mary Green is No None of us _____ Received by letter Jan as Gist Junr _____
>
> **May 10th 1805 Sunday**
> Church Met &c A door opened for Reception of Members Received by letter Abram Wood & wife Poly & John (Gist) Jas Harlin Polly Lee Brotherset at liberty Exercise her gift

(B-59)

> **May Term** *[Continued]*
>
> In Publick wherever the Lord May cast his lot John Grafton Cald to Exercise a publick a gift Saturday Received by letter John Lucas Luke Smith Brother James Harlen set apart to the office of Deacon By Ordaination Rec'd by letter John Gulley and wife by Experience Samuel Comes

> **June 8th 1805 Saturday**
>
> Church Met &c Received by letter John Gulley And his wife Elizabeth by Experience Saml Comes Appointed Brethren John Mulky Francis Baxter And John Grafton to attend the association at Mount Tabor on the 4th Saturday In July next The Church agree to send a Rem on shane against the 14th article of the last years minutes Q: the Query from Beaver creek — Also a Query to this effect — What authority have we In the word of God for a association

> **July 13th Saturday 1805**
>
> Church Met &c a door opend for the reception of members Rec'd by letter Dorcey Job, Heny Harding, Clary Harding his wife by Experience Peggy Leondra — letter to Flet[s?]n Rec'd and approbated — a charge laid in and Authenticated against Susey Strand for being married to a man that had a living wife the church declare a nonfellowship with her — turnover

July Term
Continued

Sister Nancy Gum having long absented herself from the Church and having joined another class of people — the Arians, appointed Brethren John Mulkey & Benjamin Ghest Sen. to labour with her and make Report next Meeting — Adjourned —

August 10th 1805 Saturday

Church Met &c. appointed a meeting on the last thirsday in this Inst. to look into some matters of difference. The Church agree that any member of this Society feeling a weight to exercise a public Gift are at liberty to proceed till they are either countenanced or prohibited by the Church — Bartholomew Wood and his wife — Letters of Dismission granted to —

August 31st Saturday

Church Met &c. — A charge laid against Sister Head, for Immoral Conduct, appointed Bro. Jacob & Christopher Snider to labour with her & make Report next meeting in course — Brother Mulkey & Ghest Report no satisfaction Obtained with Sister Gum — Appointed Brethren John Mulkey, Benj. Ghest Sen. and Thomas Sulivant, Frances Baxter, meson ——— —— ———— Stock —— Valley also —— Appointed Brethren Jas. Sidlock & Jno. Pinkley to labour again with Sister Gum & make Report next meeting

[Handwritten church minutes, best reading:]

September 13th 1825 — Church Met &c Brother Grider Report that Sister Heada could not attend the matter therefore laid over. Appointed Brethren Jo. Harrison and Peter Jackson to cite Br. Samuel Summers to attend next Meeting. — Appointed Brother Rich'd Pinington to cite Brother Sam'l Huff to attend next Meeting in course. The Brethren appointed to labour with Sister Guen Report no Satisfaction and she not coming forward the Church Say She is no more of us. Received by letter William Wadley.

October 15th 1825 Saturday — Church Met &c Brother Pinington Report that Br. Huff Rejects the Call of the Church He is laid under Suspension and Brethren Thomas Welch and Pinington again to cite him to next Meeting. Appointed Brother Salient to cite Br. Wm Logue to attend next Meeting. — Brother Sam Summers not coming forward appointed Brother James Harrison to cite him to attend next Meeting.

November Term 1825 — The Reference this Meeting Brother Huff taken up and laid over till next Meeting. Dismissed by letter Dorcas Job & Peggy York. Adjourn'd &c John Grastow

> **Decem 1805** — Church Met &c Brother Samuel Huff not coming forward He is therefore Declared out of the fellowship of this church and no more of us — Sister Heada come forward and as Satisfaction was not obtain'd the Church appointed Brethren Wm Wood and John Summow to labour with her and Make report Next Meeting —
>
> **January 11th 1806 Saturday** — Church Met &c Brother Ezekiel Springer with Expressing a Desire to withdraw from this church appointed Brethren Henry Hinton and Thomas Wiley to labour with him — Brother Logue come forward And by Making acknoledgement is Restored to his Recd by letter Thomas Rider and Elizabeth Rider
>
> **Febuary 8th 1806 Saturday** — Church Met &c The Reference Respecting Ezekel Springer Laid over Conversed on Some Matters & Ajourned
>
> **March 9th 1806 Saturday** — Church Met &c — The Reference Respecting Br. Ezekel Still laid Over Letters of Dismison Granted to Wm Wadley Ann Carr Polly Carr Abram Wood Polley Wood Recd by letters Jarrus Chapman & Piggy York —

> **March** **Continued**
> Appointed a Meeting on Tho 19th of This in
> to Settle Som Difficultys - Brethren Joseph Gest and
> Jas Harlen to cite Sudey Baxter to next Meeting
> Joel Moore & Thomas Wiley to cite John Gulley
>
> **March 19th Saturd**
> Church Met &c — The Reference Concerning Ezekel
> Springer Called for & he neglecting to hear the Church
> And withdrawing himself in a disorderly Maner
> We Say that he is Excluded from all previlages
> in this church and no more of us
> Brother Benjr Gest Senr to cite Thomas Gest to
> Nixt Meeting in Course
> Recd of letter John Curtis & wife
>
> **July 10th Saturd**
> Church Met &c. The Reference Concerning Susey
> Baxter Calld for and the charge against her
> (Viz pregnancy) being Authenticated the Church
> Say Say she is no more of us
> Again appointed Brethren Benjr Gest Senr
> Thomas Sulevant & Christean Frailey to labour
> with Thomas Gest and Cite him to next meeting
> Elizebeth Gulley Excluded from the church for
> Immoral conduct and Refusing to hear the church
> Brother Gulley said over

> May 9th 1806 fryday
>
> Church Met &c — The Reference Respecting Thomas Gest call'd for and he Being present and making Publick acknowledgement he is Restored to a seat.
>
> The Reference Respecting John Gulley call'd for and he not coming forward but neglecting to hear the church they say that he is no more of us ——
>
> June 14 1806 Saturday
>
> Church Met &c ——
> 1st A matter concerning Br. Wm Wood Laid in And Brethren Benjamin gist Sen'r Henry Harding Jacob grider James Harrison and Jos. Wood a committee to Enquire into the matter and make Report Next Meeting in course ——
> 2 Query what is duty to do with a member of this Church inviting men to preach at his own house or attending on the ministry of Such as we Believe to preach that which is contrary to the fundamental Doctrines of the Gospel ——
> Ans. the church Say that Such a member shall be dealt with as the Gospel directs in case of offence Adjourned &c ——

July 14 1834 Saturday

Church Met &c —— The Referance Respecting Br[o] W[illia]m Wood called for the committee Report that he confesseth the charge Just (viz the sin of adultery) the church therefor say that he is no more of us —— Appointed Brethren James Harlin and Benjamin Rush to cite Walter Homes to attend next meeting

August 9 1834 Saturday

Church met and after Sermon by Br[o] V Burton a door opend for Reception Rec[eive]d by letter John Davis Elizabeth davis his wife, and the Referance Regarding Br[o] Homes call for & he not coming forward the church again agreed to send Brethren Jn[o] Ellison John Curtis to labour with him & cite him to next meeting —— Agreed to consideration of the Scriptural authority of an assossiation and converse thereon next meeting in course ——

11. Church Met &c — A door opend for Reception of members Rec[eive]d By letter Bartholomew Wood & wife — the Grice concerning Walter Homes called for the committee Report no satisfaction and he not comming forward But refusing to hear the church therefore say he is no more of us

> continued Appointed Brother John Mulkey John Wood Christian Frailey to attend the Association on the fourth Saturday in this Inst at Roaring River Meeting house A dismission granted to Br John Lucas — The Bill Brought Before the Church concerning the Building The Meeting house appointed Bro James Harrison & Phillip Breant to vote the Same and Make Report next meeting
>
> October 10 1806 ydoy
>
> Church Met &c — a door open for Reception Recd B. ... tation Brother John Sivey the Report concerning the meeting house called for and Refered Bro Jno Gondra Expressing to the church an Impression og d to excuse the Church agree that he may on Trial at this Place —
> Joel Moore Suspended from Priviledge Appointed Bro Francis Baxter & J. Gist Labour with him and cite him to next Meeting

Old Mulkey: A Pioneer Plea for the Ancient Order

> Mon
> 3rd
> 1806
> Saturday
>
> Church Met &c adj'nd open for Reception of Members Rec'd by Letter Abram Hestand his wife Elizabeth – The Reference concerning the Building the meeting house call'd for And settled agreeable to the Judgement of James Harrison & Phillip Bruant The Respecting Joel moore call'd for and Agreed to Meet on friday preceding next m[eeting] Provets ly to converse on same m[eeting] –––
>
> December
> 18th
> 1816
>
> Church Met &c The Reference concerning Joel Moore call'd for the Brethren no Satisfaction obtain'd But Persiteing in Contimoneing Doctrine to The Gospel and Refuseing With the Call and Request of Church we therefore Say that he is no more of us

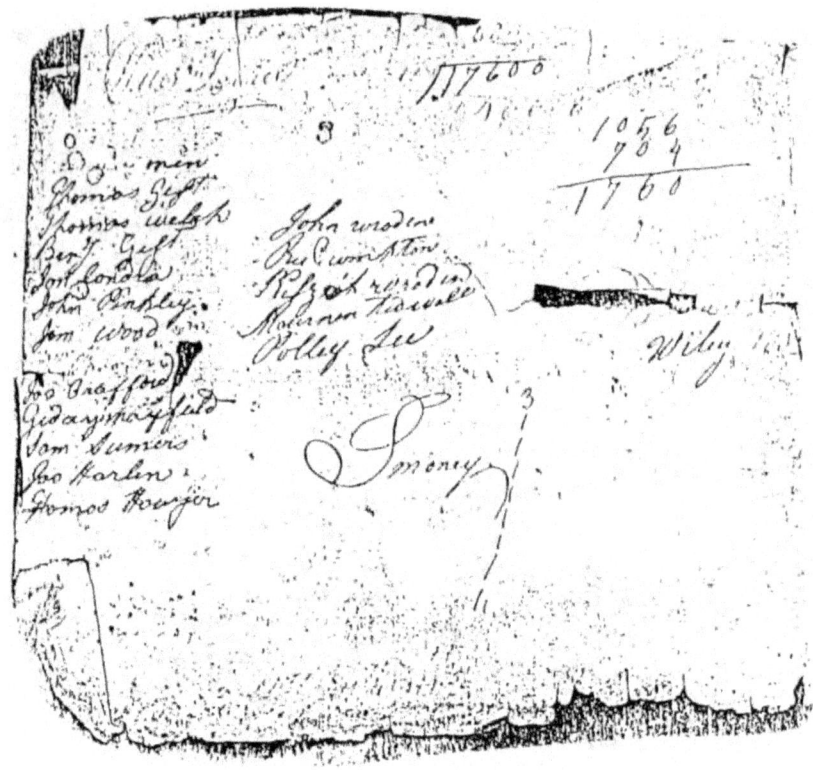

(B-70)

Church Met &c (P)

August Second Saturday 1809 — 1st Charges Exibited against Brother John Mulkey, in Consequence of which the church agreed to send for help to assist us in our October meeting.

October Second Saturday 1809 — Church met agreeable to appointment, with the help sent proceeded to hear the charges against Brother Mulkey with other's help of which time and then again hearing the charges Exibited and received we then concluded that he denied the _____ Gentiles ___ of the Gospel as denying in our Esteem that Jesus Christ satisfy the demands of Law and Justice for his people by direct action ____ or that any man is saved by the Righteousness of Jesus Christ imputed to us only for ____ the church with contempt And going away and leaving us in our ____

November ___ Saturday 1809 — church met and adiction took place, and those whose names are above written declared that they would no longer remain under the ____ of this church ____ with drawd from us consequently are ____ of us.

(B-72)

A History of the Mill Creek ("Old Mulkey") Church
Tompkinsville, Kentucky

Appendix C

Miscellaneous

The Old Minute Book

The earliest existing Church records of *"Old Mulkey"* or *"Mill Creek Church"* as it was called at that time, go back to September 11, 1798, the date of the first minutes in the first book - according to tradition, earlier records written in pokeberry ink on a parchment scroll were lost or accidentally destroyed.

On the inside cover of the first church book is the inscription:

"A Book Of Records for the Church of Mill Creek, William Marrs Logue." [The opposite page contains these words,] *"A Book of Records for the Church of Christ on the head of Big Barron Mill Creek, William Marrs Logue. Made July 11, 1799, Church book 1799. Philip Mulkey, Clerk."*

The old church covenant and a copy of the Constitution of the Green River Association of Baptist are in the first part of the book. This list of members is also listed in the front of the old Church Book.[1]

Old Membership List

Benjamin Rush, Aaron Hays, William M. Logue, James Harrison, Tolly Thompson, Ribba Kerby, Bathsheba Nelson, Joel Nelson, Grace Rush, Salley Nelson, Thomas Welch, Ester Harden, Ephriam Duhen, Valentine Harlen, Ester Sulivant, Jacob Groder, William Wood, Sarah Wood, Obadiah Howard, Alice Means, Sally Lane, Mary Waldrop, Mary Green, Issac Means, Senr., Samuel Wood, Susannah Means, Joel Moore, Ann Carr, Rachel Rush, Sarrah White, Labon Ellis, Lydia Vaughn, Nancy Patterson, Becky Lewis, Stephen Howard, Thomas Wood, Nickolus Howser, Jane Howser, Phillip Briant, Robert Lane, Mary Lane, Peter Jackson, Margaret Jackson, Joshua McFerson, Frances Baxter, Poley Gates, Elizabeth Brownen, Rebekeh Brownen, Betey B. Brownen, Betey Howard, Mary Denant, John Summers, Nancy Summers, John Condra.

Poley Got, Phebe Lions, Christopher Howard, William Summers, Polley Ward, Salley Smith, William Codel, Talman Lane, Knelly Grider, Travis Wm. Chism, Nancy Thompson, Nancy Lok, Polly Dickerson, Susey Stroud, Henry King, Elizabeth King, Jude Elles, Jacob Chism, James Baxter, Nancy Clerk, John Springer, Poley Springer, Dienah Anderson, Nancy Howser, William Pohon, Peggy York, Hannah Gist Junr., Abram Wood, Polley Wood, John Grasta, Samuel Harlan, Polly Lee, John Lucus, Lucke Smith, John Gulley, Elizabeth Gulley, Samuel Comer, Jude Headda, Dorcas Jobe, Henry Harding, Clara Harding, Peggy Condra, William Wadley, Thomas Rider, Elizabeth Rider, James Chapman, Peggy York, John Curtis, Hannah Curtis, John Daves, Bartholomew Wood, Elizabeth Wood.

---

[1] Many of the names are obviously misspelled, and the poor condition of the manuscript makes others hard to determine.

John Mulkey, John Wood, Thas, Sulivant, Hannah Gist, Mary Chism, Rachel Collins, John Compton, Nancy Compton, Thomas Wood, Ezekiel Springer, Rebekah Springer, Nancy Gum, Isabel Bushong, Sarah Morris, Isabel Sumers, Samuel Sumers, Richd. Pennington, Hannah Pennington, Joseph Gist, Nathan Breed, Benjamin Gist Junr.; Mary Gist, Senr., Susannah Cumens, Ledia Marrs, Samuel Huff, Jarret White, James Harlen, Eda Harlen, Betey Wood, Senr.; Betey Wood, Junr.; Daniel Heaslen, Samuel Vaughen, Abram Hesten, Rebeka Willa, Regena Moore, Kenzy Tuddor, James Rush, Gideon Mayfield, Jane Proctor, Molley Rush, Robert Kerby, Francis Ray, Salley Boiles, Frankey Scott, Sarrah Sulivant, Richard Compton, Isaac Means, Junr., Thomas Wila, John Pinkley, Ruth Homes, Christn Frailey, Walter Homes, John Wooden, Keziah Warden, Mourner Tidwell, John Sims, William Huff.

* * *

Soldiers of the Revolution

The following Soldiers of the Revolution are buried in the old church yard:

Nathan Breed, Liuet., Woods County, Va., Mil. Rev. War.
John Rasner, Pvt., Neville's Va, Reg.
Thomas White, Born 1758 in Ireland- died 1835.
Edward Pediford, Pvt., 3 Va. Reg.
Obadiah Howard, SC. Mil.
Luke Metheaney, Pvt., Grayson's Reg.
John Morehead, Pvt., Tripletts Un. Co.
Thos. Bartley, Pvt., 3 M.C. Reg.
Thos Brown, Drum Major, 14 Va. Reg.

Fleming Smith, Pvt., Thos. S.C. Troops
John Giles, Sgt., Locke's Reg.
Soloman Dickerson, Pvt., Griffin's M.D. Reg.
Matthew Kidwell, Pvt., Hanson's Med. Reg.
Joseph Gist, Indian Spy, Seviers N.D. Reg.
John Gist, Va. State Troops

Main Cemetery

Following are the names, dates of birth, dates of death, epitaphs, etc.; taken from the stones in the cemetery in the churchyard at Old Mulkey.

Beals, Isaac Feb. 25, 1805-Nov. 15, 1882

Beals, Annie June 23, 1808-Sept 12, 1890

Breed, Mary Harlan, wife of Nathan Breed 1748 in Pa. to Aaron and Sarah Harlan

Breed, Nathan Lieut. Woods Co., Va. Mil. Rev. War Bartley, Thomas Pvt. 3 MD Regt. Rev. War

Brown, Thomas Drum Major 14 Va. Regt. Rev. War

Boone, Squire born in Penn. Oct. 5, 1744, died in Ind. Built Travelers Rest

Boone, Hannah (sister of Daniel Boone) Born in Berks County, Pa. Aug 24, 1746 Died in Monroe County, Ky. 1828

Conner, Lawrence Pvt. Camp Bell's, Va. Regt. Rev. War March 17, 1826

Chism, James Pvt. L. Va. Regt. Rev. War

Depp, William Pvt. Harris Co.,Va. Troops Rev. War Oct. 19, 1834

Emmert, Eld. Phillip Mar. 10, 1795-June 5, 1859 "Our Father has gone to a mansion of rest to the glorius land by the Diety Blest"

Emmert, William J. Co. B-9th Ky. Inf.

Gist, Joseph Kentucky Indian spy N.C. Regt. Rev. War

Graven, Matilda G. Oct. 21 1836- June 5, 1870 Wife of C M . Graven

Gee, Julia D. Sept. 16, 1865-March 7, 1867

Gee, Sally T. - Jan. 30, 1851-Aug.23, 1856 Daughter of John J. and Elizabeth B. Gee

Gee, Taswell T. Sept. 19, 1845-May 23, 1877 Son of J.J. and E.B.

Gee Taswell Thou has left us. Thy loss we deeply feel. This God that has us. But he can all our sorrows heal.

Gee, Elizabeth B. Mar. 21, 1828-Jan. 30, 1878 Wife of J.J. Gee. Here lies one who in this life was a kind mother, a true wife.

Giles, John, Sgt. Lockes Regt. Rev. War.

Giss, John Virginia State Troops Rev. War.

Hix, Greenbeery Nov. 29, 1817-Sept. 6, 1865 (Greenberry Hix and Nancy Hix were Great Grandparents of Mrs. Pearl Eagle Bushong)

Howard, William G. May 11, 1804-Nov. 9, 1830. Sacred.

Howard, Christopher 1775 His wife, Rebecca Hayes. Erected by Guy and Mont Corner and Alex Harlin.

Howard, Mary 1760 Married 1778 to James Chism Pvt. 2 Va. Regt.

Howard, Jessee 1795-1852

Howard, Lucy Mayfield 1798-1861. Wife of Jessee Howard.

Howard, Harmond Feb. 11, 1794-April 26, 1855

Howard, Obadiah S.C. Mil. Rev. War

Howard, Priscilla Avery Breed 1742-1808 Wife of Obadiah Howard.

Howard, Aunt Rachel Lived 102 years. Slave to her mistress.

Howard, William March 4, 1772-Oct. 8, 1848. In Memory.

Howard, Jane 1772-Jan. 24, 1855. In Memory.

Howard, Ellis Born and died July 30, 1885 Son of J.L. and A.M. Howard. "Free from all cares and pain; Asleep my baby lies; Until the final trumpet call the dead to Christ."

Kidwell, Matthew Pvt. Hansons M.D. Regt. Rev. War 1842

Metheany, Luke Pvt. Grayson Va. Regt. Rev. War. Aug. 4, 1839

Morehead, John Pvt. Trippletts Va. Co. Rev. Aug 1845

Mulkey, Eld. J.N. Departed this life Sept. 26, 1882 Age 76 yrs, 7 m's and 15 days. "Why lament the Christians dying; Why indulge in his tears of gloom; Calmly on his Lord relying; He was met the opening tomb; Hark, the golden harps are ringing; Sounds celestial fill his ear; millions now in heaven singing; Greet his joyful entrance in."

Monroe, John Pvt. 5 Va. Regt. Rev. War. Philpott, Emley Hunter Wife of L.E . Philpott Philpott, Dora (no dates)

Pediford, Edward Pvt. # Virginia Regt. Rev. War. Died 1835.

Propliet, Jerry 8-9- - 1-29-1848

Rasner, John Pvt. Nevilles Va. Regt. Rev. War. Feb. 24, 1844

Smith, Fleming Pvt. Thomas S.C. Troops Rev. War.

Thomas, Talbert 1780-1834

Thomas, Elizabeth Breed 1790-1825. Wife of Talbert Thomas. Thomas, William Howard 1830-1864 Son of Talbert Thomas.

Thomas, Eleanor Y. Howard June 20, 1807-Jan. 28, 1863. Wife of Tolbert Thomas.

Thomas, John C. March 3,1831-Oct. 8,1835. "In memory of."

Thomas, Samuel 1796-1882

Thomas, Sarah Northcross 1800 Wife of Samuel Thomas.

Wilson, Gen'l Samuel Dec. 6, 1775-Dec. 6, 1831. "Patented and gave this ground for a church." Married Elizabeth Hughlett.

White, Thomas Born 1758 in Ireland about 1835 Soldier in Rev. War. Private (cook) under Gen. Francis Marion. "Prepared and served to Gen. Marion and British officers the famous dinner of Potatoes."

* * *

The New Meetinghouse

According to history, the first meetinghouse of the Mill Creek Baptist Church was located on the banks of Mill Creek, some 200 yards from the present structure.

In April, 1804, a committee of seven men was appointed to make plans for building a new meetinghouse. John Wood, Nathan Breed, James Harlin, Ephriam Ellis, Francis Baxter, Joseph Gist, and Thomas Sullivan were named to the committee.[2]

The next month the committee reported that the building was to be 50 feet long, 30 feet wide, shingled with jointed shingles, and including five windows and three doors; a man was to be hired and paid in trade by subscription.[3]

The man that was hired to build the meetinghouse was Jiles Thompson, or his agents.[4]

The building is built with 12 corners and in the shape of a cross with three doors. Many historians believe that the 12 corners represent the 12 apostles, while others believe they represent the 12 tribes of Israel. The three doors are said to be symbolic of the Holy Trinity,[5]

Services continued to be held regularly in the Old Mulkey Meetinghouse until about 1856.

The Tompkinsville Church of Christ was constituted on November 27, 1841,[6] and those members that left Old Mulkey around 1856 reportedly moved their membership there.[7]

In the late 1870's, some of the local residents, including John Gee and Frank Pedigo, who had close historical, sentimental ties with the old church, took charge of a renovation of the Old Mulkey Meetinghouse. Rails were split for the erection of a fence around the old church graveyard, and a new clapboard roof was installed on the old meetinghouse which had stood

---

[2] *Minutes of the Mill Creek Baptist Church*, (April 12, 1804), p. 49
[3] *Ibid*, (May 11, 1804), p. 50.
[4] *Ibid*, (November 10, 1804), p. 54.
[5] *Old Mulkey Meetinghouse State Historic Site*, pamphlet distributed at Old Mulkey.
[6] *Minutes of the Tompkinsville Church of Christ*, (November 1841).
[7] *Old Mulkey Meetinghouse State Historic Site*, pamphlet distributed at Old Mulkey.

neglected since the mid- 1850's. Following this renovation, the grounds again stood neglected for more than a decade, and at one point a fire swept the area destroying the fence.

W. S. Emmert and Newton M. Ray spearheaded a drive in 1890 to restore the meetinghouse and the cemetery. After the renovation was completed, weekly religious meetings and community singings were held in the Old Mulkey Meetinghouse and there were occasional preaching services conducted. But the building fell into disuse and was again abandoned about 1910.

In the summer of 1925, the Honorable Joe H. Eagle, a United State Representative from Houston and a Monroe County native, visited the Old Mulkey Meetinghouse with a Reverend Willie Thomas of Tompkinsville.

Eagle reported to the local newspaper:

> "Will and I found the old Meeting House with the roof off, the doors and windows gone, a sad looking picture of neglect. We decided to try to save it. We knew the people would do it if called to their attention. So we gave our checks for $50 each to start the fund, and the good people who felt the same way put the old historic structure in repair."

Once a board of trustees was established, public donations were made to rebuild and restore the building to its original condition. The public responded to the cause and sufficient funds were raised. New sleepers were laid, and on them were laid a new puncheon floor. Split-log seats with peg-legs were added, just as in the original meetinghouse, and the wooden shutters fashioned after the original ones were placed over the windows. Thus, within the framework of the original logs, the structure was restored in every respect to its 1804 form.

It was only fitting that in November 1931, this pioneer structure with its adjoining cemetery was declared one of Kentucky's State Parks for perpetuation as an historical and religious site.[8]

---

[8] *Old Mulkey Meetinghouse Stale Historic Site*, pamphlet distributed at Old Mulkey.

The Old Mulkey Meetinghouse State Shrine was declared a Kentucky State Park in 1931 in a formal dedication led by Governor Flem D. Sampson.[9]

* * *

Hannah Boone

Of all the graves in the old churchyard at Old Mulkey, the most notable is probably that of Hannah Boone, sister of the famous Kentucky explorer, Daniel Boone.

Hannah Boone was married to John Stewart. Stewart was a pioneer and companion of Daniel Boone, on his first trip to Kentucky in 1760.

Hannah was the youngest daughter of Squire Boone and Sarah Morgan. She was born in Berks County, Pennsylvania in 1746. In 1750-1751, her parents moved to Rowan County, North Carolina and she was married to John Stewart in 1765.

John Stewart came back to Kentucky with Daniel Boone and four other hunters: Joseph Holden, James Mooney, William Cooley, and John Findley in 1769. They crossed the mountains at Cumberland Gap and made their first camp, called Station Camp, on the Kentucky River.

Stewart and Boone were captured while on a hunt by a large party of Shawnee Indians who forced them to lead the party back to their camp. The Indians robbed the camp of all furs, supplies, and horses leaving them with little ammunition. Stewart and Boone followed the Indians and were able to escape with two horses during the night. Two days later, Stewart and Boone were captured again when the Indians discovered their loss. Sometime between January and May of 1770, Stewart was killed by the Indians. Later when blazing the Wilderness Trail, Boone found Stewart's remains in a

---

[9] Loy Milam, "The Old Mulkey Meeting House State Shrine," (January/February 1983 issue of *Back Home in Kentucky*), pp. 24-25.

hollow sycamore tree. It was apparent that Stewart had been wounded and had hidden in the tree where he bled to death.

After the death of John Stewart, Hannah Boone married Richard Pennington in North Carolina around 1776. They came to Kentucky, but finally settled at Sparta in White County, Tennessee. After the death of Richard in 1813, Hannah moved to the home of her son, Daniel Boone Pennington, in Monroe County, Kentucky where she died in 1828 at the age of 82. Tradition holds that Hannah Boone Pennington was among the members that went out the west door with John Mulkey and the majority in the split of the Mill Creek Baptist Church on November 18, 1804.[10]

* * *

---

[10] *Old Mulkey Meetinghouse State Historic Site*, pamphlet distributed at Old Mulkey.

A History of the Mill Creek ("Old Mulkey") Church
Tompkinsville, Kentucky

Appendix D

Bibliography

Benedict, *A History of the Baptist Denomination in America*, 2 volumes.

Boles, James B., *Religion in Antebellum Kentucky*.

Campbell, Alexander, *Millennial Harbinger*, (1830-1870).

Campbell, Alexander, *The Christian Baptist*, (1823-1829).

Cawthorn, Warnell, *Pioneer Baptist Church Records of South- Central Kentucky and the Upper Cumberland of Tennessee 1799- 1899*.

Court Order Book No. 1, Barren County, Kentucky 1799-1802. Crismon, Leo Taylor, *Baptists in Kentucky*, 1776-1976, *A Bicentennial Volume*.

Goode, Cecil, L. Gardner, Jr., Woodford, *Barren County Heritage*. Gooden, E. Clayton, *A Fork in the Road.*

Gooden, E. Clayton, "Old Mulkey Church Was One Of Sate's Earliest Pioneer Churches", January, 1965 issue of the *Discipliana*, reprinted in *The Kentucky Explorer*, February, 1993.

Gooden, E. Clayton, *"The Old Mulkey Meeting House, John Mulkey: The Man With A Majority."*

Hailey, Homer, *Attitudes and Consequences In The Restoration Movement.*

Haynes, Nathaniel S., *History of the Disciples of Christ in Illinois.*

History of the Fitzgeralds and Geralds (private printing).

Masters, Frank M., *A History of Baptists in Kentucky.*

Milam, Loy, *"The Old Mulkey Meeting House State Shrine,"* (January/February 1983 issue of *Back Home in Kentucky*).

Milam, Loy, *The Restoration Messenger,* printed weekly in the *Tompkinsville News*, Tompkinsville, Kentucky, beginning in late 1995.

Minutes of Big Pigeon Baptist Church, 1787-1874, Cocke County, Tennessee.

Minutes of Dripping Spring Baptist Church.

Minutes of Green River Association.

Minutes of the Mil l Creek Baptist Church.

Minutes of the Mil l Creek Baptist Church No. 2.

Minutes of the Mt. Tabor Baptist Church. Minutes of the Stockton Valley Association.

Mulkey, John, *"A Circular Letter Addressed to the Christian Churches in the Western Country"* [printed by] J.A. Woodson, Glasgow, Ky. 1821, (Copy in Christian Theological Seminary Library, Indianapolis, IN).

Old Mulkey Meetinghouse State Historic Site, small pamphlet distributed at Old Mulkey.

Renau, Isaac T., "Obituary," *Christian Review*, Vol. II, No. 5 (May 1845), p.120.

Richardson, Robert, *Memoirs of Alexander Campbell*, 2 volumes.

Rogers, W.C., *Recollections of Men of Faith*.

Spencer, J. H., *History of Kentucky Baptist*, 2 volumes.

Stone, Barton W., *Biography of Elder Barton Warren Stone*.

Stone, Barton W., *Christian Messenger*, (1826-1845).

The Mulkeys of America, (private printing, 1982).

Tompkinsville Church of Christ, *Congregational History*, Bulletin printed, November 16, 1986.

West, Earl Irving, *Elder Ben Franklin: Eye of the Storm*.

West, Earl Irving, *The Search for the Ancient Order*, 4 volumes.

Williams, John A., *Life of Elder John Smith*.

Notes

Notes

Notes

Notes

Notes

www.ingramcontent.com/pod-product-compliance
Lightning Source LLC
Chambersburg PA
CBHW071901290426
44110CB00013B/1235